YES OR NO?

Yes or No?

Straight Answers to Tough Questions about Christianity

by

Peter Kreeft

IGNATIUS PRESS   SAN FRANCISCO

Originally published by
Servant Publications
Ann Arbor, Michigan

Cover by Kelly Connelly

Published 1991, Ignatius Press, San Francisco
© 1984 Peter Kreeft
All rights reserved
ISBN 0-89870-358-1
Library of Congress catalogue card number 90-85102
Printed in the United States of America

Contents

for Pat and Roger Verhulst

Introduction

"YES OR NO?" WHAT A TITLE! So black-or-white!

But life presents us with nothing black or white. The title seems unrealistic, irrelevant to life.

Wrong. Life does present us with some things that are black or white. Here are two of them: black and white.

More seriously, here are two more: Heaven and Hell.

Oh, but they're not part of *life*, you say. Well, if they aren't, then Christianity is simply false. The choice for or against God, the choice to believe or not to believe, to hope in God or not to hope, to love or not to love—that choice makes an eternal and infinite difference. That is the stark and wonderful news Christianity brings us. If it is true, it is the most important truth we have ever been told. If it is false, it is the biggest lie we have ever been told. And it is the duty of every honest person to try to find out which it is.

This book is written to help you make the most important choice of your life. The choice is simple, but the reasons for and against it are not.

The choice is simple because it is a choice between saying "yes" or "no" to God as we meet him in Jesus. "Yes" is the simplest word there is.

The reasons for and against Christianity are not simple because Christianity is full of wonderful mysteries which are as far above the power of the human mind to grasp fully as Beethoven or Einstein are far above the power of a clam to grasp.

I do not claim to have proved everything in this book beyond doubt. Doubt is always possible wherever faith is free, just as hate is always possible where love is free. Faith is not the opposite of doubt; faith can include doubt. The opposite of faith is not doubt but indifference, just as the opposite of love is not hate (love can include hate) but indifference.

Pascal, who wrote brilliantly "against indifference" in his *Pensées*, said that there are only three kinds of people in the world:

1. those who have sought God and found him;
2. those who have sought him and not yet found him;
3. those who neither seek him nor find him.

Jesus promised, "Everyone who seeks, finds." So everyone in the second class winds up in the first class. The great divide, then, is between seekers and non-seekers (the indifferent).

This book is for seekers.

It is called *Yes or No?* because there are three possible answers to every question: "yes", "no", and evasion. To some questions, evasion is a possible answer, but not to a marriage proposal. Christianity is God's marriage proposal to the soul. And death makes evasion impossible.

This book is designed to be used in two different ways:

1. by Pascal's three types of individuals:

a. For those of you who have already refused evasion and sought God and also have found him, this book is to strengthen your faith and help you obey the Bible's command to "be prepared to give a reason for the hope that is in you";

b. For those who have not yet found him and are still seeking, this book is a road map;

c. For those who have not yet bothered to seek, this book is an alarm clock: an attempt to wake you up and inveigle you to at least ask the greatest questions in the world, questions about who you are and why you are and what your life means;

2. by classes in religious education.

I teach religion and philosophy in college. I have asked hundreds of students about their religious education in high school, and I have been shocked.

I have been shocked first at the results. It made ex-Christians out of many.

I have been shocked, second, at the textbooks. They are a disaster area. Almost all of them seem to have been written by Job's three friends, or perhaps by some official in Hell's hierarchy of demons for the express purpose of boring people away from the Faith. For they were almost always vague and dull, two things Christianity certainly is not. If anyone says Christianity is a crazy, spectacular fairy tale—well, at least that person sees that it is spectacular. But if anyone says it's dull, he simply hasn't looked at it. It's not usually his fault: nobody ever showed him the real thing. He was given platitudes instead, a candle instead of a volcano.

Third, I have been shocked at the attitudes of some of the teachers. Many were good, conscientious people who did their best. But others seemed to be as bored as the students. And many were afraid of questions. That shocked me most. I think a good teacher must love questions. For the only way really to learn an answer is really to ask a question. There is nothing more dead and irrelevant than an answer to a question that has never been asked.

Questions express interest, and will—the will to know. This is infinitely precious, because it is (at least unconsciously) a search for God under his attribute of truth. This is the only honest reason why anyone should ever believe Christianity, or anything else: because it is true. It may also be helpful, comforting, challenging, relevant, responsible, creative, or dozens of other things; but none of those is the first reason why an honest person believes Christianity. They are the bloom on the rose of truth, the icing on the cake of truth. Too many books are all icing.

This book (which is the first in a series) is meant to be different. For one thing, it is written in the form of dialogues, conversations between two people, to encourage the reader to enter the conversation and ask the hard questions, the great questions. They also try to guide the questioner fairly and freely to the answers God has given us in his Word; that is, his Book, and above all his Son. (Both are called "the Word of God").

One of the two people in these dialogues, Sal, is not a Christian but is an honest and open-minded questioner ("Sal the seeker"). The other, Chris, is a Christian who tries to answer Sal's hard questions. Notice that "Sal" can be for "Sally" or "Salvatore" and "Chris" can be for "Christopher" or "Christine". You can imagine them as boys, girls, women, or men.

Another way in which this book is meant to be different is that it does not use its readers as guinea pigs to test the latest innovation in theology or psychology. It merely serves up the basics of the Faith that has been the food of Christian souls for nearly 2,000 years. The proof of the pudding is in the eating. We need not an instant-processed, fast-food Christianity but "the beef", not Christianity-and-water but "mere Christianity". (The phrase comes from C. S. Lewis, and so do many of the ideas in this book.) There is plenty of "Christianity-and" around, especially in the religious education books: Christianity-and-legalism, Christianity-and-modern-psychology, Christianity-and-Marxism, Christianity-and-Capitalism, Christianity and the latest patronizing attempt to "sell" Christianity to the modern mind by chopping off its unfashionable corners or filling in its mysterious depths.

"But you can't turn back the clock. Modernity and secularism are here to stay."

That's not what God said. He promised that the gates of Hell would not prevail against his Church. Why should the world be able to do what Hell itself is unable to do?

And as for turning back the clock, you certainly can! If a clock is keeping the wrong time, the only way to make progress is by turning it back to the true time. Billy Graham was once criticized for turning back the clock 200 years. He replied that if he had done that, he had failed, for he was trying to turn it back 2,000 years.

No idea is put forward in this book because it is old *or* because it is new, but only because it is true.

One of the questions I asked hundreds of students was: "What do you want in a religious education course, or text-book?" One of the most frequent answers was: "Relevance to my life". I agree with that demand; if a thing makes no *difference* to your life, why bother with it? But I do not agree with the way most textbooks try to meet that de-mand. They water Christianity down. They emphasize the easy parts, the parts no one disagrees with, like being ma-ture and responsible and compassionate and loving your neighbor. But we know that already, essential as it is. What more does Christianity tell us? What did God tell us that we didn't already know?

To make Christianity relevant to our lives, we must first know what Christianity *is*. Here, then, is some hard think-ing about the shocking glory, the startling story that is "the greatest story ever told".

Dialogue One

Why Believe?

Sal the Seeker: Where are we?

Chris the Christian: In a book.

Sal: What? What are we doing there?

Chris: We're characters in a dialogue—a fictional conversation invented by some author.

Sal: What kind of a book is it?

Chris: A book about religion.

Sal: Ugh. Is it as bad as that? We're really stuck, then.

Chris: But this isn't like other religion books.

Sal: Why not?

Chris: It's a dialogue. *Two* points of view are here, not just one.

What is a dialogue?

Sal: Two points of view? What are they?

Chris: You're one; I'm the other.

Sal: Why?

Chris: The dialogue form is meant to stimulate questioning, exploring, thinking things out for yourself.

Sal: Well, that's an improvement. Maybe this book *will* be different. Where did the author get this idea, writing in dialogue form instead of just lecturing or preaching?

Chris: It's a very old idea. A man named Socrates in ancient Greece invented it. He was our first great philosopher. It's called the Socratic Method.

Sal: Philosophy? That sounds pretty difficult. Are we going to discuss philosophy?

Chris: No.

Sal: Religion, then?

Chris: No, Christianity.

The question: What difference Christianity makes

Sal: What's the difference?

Chris: That's what we're here to find out: What makes Christianity different.

Sal: You know, I don't believe in all that stuff.

Chris: I know. That's why you're here. You and I make a good pair for a dialogue. We're not the same.

Sal: I wonder about that. I think we *are* the same in every really important way. We're both human beings. We both live and die and laugh and cry and love and think. We both have a conscience and a set of values. Isn't it enough just to be a good person and lead a good life? Isn't that the most important thing? Can't you live just as good a life without being a Christian?

Chris: You wonder what difference Christianity makes.

Sal: Yes.

Chris: That depends on what you think Christianity is. If you think it's just going to church on Sunday and taking a few religion classes, then I agree with you— that alone doesn't make a tremendous difference. But I think Christianity does make a tremendous difference. So I think there's a lot more to Christianity than just being in church and religion class.

Sal: Why? Non-Christians can have good values too, and live a good life. You don't need Christianity to have a conscience, or to love your neighbor.

Chris: I agree.

Sal: So why bother with Christianity then? What will it do for me?

Chris: You would believe it only if it did something for you?

Sal: Why else?

Chris: I think there's only one honest reason for anyone ever to believe anything.

Sal: What's that?

Chris: Because it's true. Do you think it's honest to believe something that isn't true?   *Honesty*

Sal: No . . .

Chris: Even if it does you some good?

Sal: I don't want to believe lies. Santa Claus might do me some good if I believed in him, but I won't believe in him if he isn't real. And I think God is like Santa Claus. Believing might make you a better person, but if he isn't really there, then I don't want to believe in him.

Chris: Good for you.

Sal: What? I thought you'd criticize me for not believing in God.

Chris: I think you're wrong about God, but you're right about honesty. I'll never say you should believe something that isn't true just because it will make you good. I believe Christianity because I believe it's true. It claims to be the truth about God and about us, not just ethical advice about how to live.

Sal: Christianity *claims* to be the truth, yes. But how do you know it *is* the truth?

Chris: That's the big question we're here to discuss. This first dialogue is only to get the *question* straight.   *Get the question straight*

Sal: Do you think you can prove it's true?

Chris: I think I can prove some of it, and I think I can give good reasons for believing even the parts I can't prove, and I think I can answer your objections to it.

Sal: Give me an example. You're getting pretty abstract.

Chris: All right. I think I can prove there is a God, but I don't think anyone can prove God is a Trinity, three persons. But I think I can show you that it's not a contradiction for one God to be three persons.

Sal: How can you prove there is a God?

Chris: Stick around.

Sal: And you said you had good reasons for believing what you couldn't prove, like the Trinity. Well, give me a good reason for believing that.

Chris: I'll give you three: Jesus, the Bible, and the Church all say so.

Sal: That's not reason, that's authority.

Chris: Don't you believe the moon is smaller than the earth?

Sal: Of course, but why change the subject? What in the world does that have to do with believing in the Trinity?

Chris: Can you prove the moon is smaller?

Sal: No, but the scientists can.

Chris: And you believe the scientists, right?

Sal: Sure.

Authority   *Chris:* So you accept their authority.

Sal: Well, they're good scientists. They have a right to say.

Chris: That's right. Authority doesn't mean power, or being the boss. It means having the right to say. It's right, not might. A good scientist has the right to tell us how big the moon is, and we have good reason to believe him, right?

Sal: Yes. But scientists can make mistakes.

Chris: Yes. All human authorities are fallible. They can make mistakes. But if there is a God, his authority would be infallible. God doesn't make mistakes.

Sal: If there is a God.

Chris: Yes. And *if* Jesus is the Son of God and *if* the Church is his teaching institution, and *if* the Bible is inspired by God, then these three are authorities.

Sal: If. If. If. That's three big ifs there.

Chris: Yes, they are. And I'll try to prove all three to you in other dialogues. All I want to show you now is that we all believe many things because we trust authorities. You believe Paris exists even though you've never been there because you trust the authorities, the travel books and photographs and the travellers.

Sal: Right. So what?

Chris: That's why I believe God is a Trinity. The authorities say so.

Sal: But you haven't proved the authorities are right.

Chris: Not yet, not to you. But I decided to believe, myself, and I can tell you my reasons. Maybe you'll agree with them, maybe not.

Sal: You mean you're going to try to argue me into Christianity?

Chris: No, I can just show you some of the evidence, some of the reasons, that's all. You have to decide for yourself.

Sal: All right, just as long as we get that straight. I want to be left free to think for myself, not be pressured by some religion pusher.

Chris: Good. I think everyone should decide for himself, freely, whether to believe or not. But to do that, you have to look at the evidence honestly and open-mindedly and fairly.

Sal: Is that why you chose to believe? Didn't your parents teach you?

Chris: Of course. But when we grow up we have to make up our own minds. I chose to believe, and that choice was just as free for me as your choice not to believe was your free choice.

Sal: Did you look at everything in Christianity before you decided? It must take a lifetime to go over every teaching one by one.

Chris: Of course not. Do you work out every equation in astronomy before you choose to believe the things the astronomers tell you? No, you decide to trust the astronomers, then you believe the things they tell you on their authority. So I decided to trust God's messengers, then believed what they tell us.

Sal: God's messengers? What do you mean?

Chris: Jesus, and then his disciples who wrote the New Testament and were the first Church.

Sal: Isn't there a big difference between Protestants and Catholics on how the Church comes into it?

Chris: Yes, but the difference is not as big as you might think. Both accept the Church and the Bible as authorities. But Protestants don't believe the Church is infallible, and Catholics do.

Sal: What's the difference between Protestants and Catholics about the Bible?

Chris: Some Protestants don't even believe the Bible is infallible. But those who do, put the Bible before the Church. They believe the Church should be judged by the Bible.

Sal: How do Catholics argue differently?

Chris: They believe the Church wrote the Bible, so if the Bible is infallible the Church has to be infallible too. How could a fallible cause produce an infallible effect?

Sal: Those are tricky arguments. Do you mind if we skip them for now? I'm not that interested in arguments between Protestants and Catholics yet. I'm trying to decide whether this whole thing of Christianity is true or not.

Chris: Good. You're putting the questions straight. First things first. And you're also asking the right question, the honest question, "Is it *true*?" not "Do I like it?" or "Will it make me feel good?" or even "Will it help me?"

Sal: I'm glad you feel that way. If something isn't true, I don't want to believe it even if it helps me. I know believing in God helps a lot of people, and I was a little afraid to share my doubts with you because I thought I might seem cruel to tell you that you were believing a fairy tale. Like Santa Claus: you don't want to tell a little kid there's no Santa Claus because it would be cruel. But you have to be honest.

Chris: Yes, and you do tell children when they get older and want to know the truth. That's where we are now: old enough to want to know whether the things our parents and teachers told us are true.

Sal: I'm glad we agree about the question, at least.

Chris: So am I. Now we can go *together* to look at Christianity's claim to be the answer.

Sal: I hope whoever is reading us feels the same way, because if they do, then they're really exploring along with us. Otherwise they're just reading words. But don't you think they'll be afraid to think about these questions?

Chris: Why?

Sal: Won't they be afraid of losing their faith?

Chris: If they feel that way, they don't have much faith in the first place. If you're confident of something, you welcome honest questions about it.

Sal: I'm really glad to hear you say that. I thought believers just blocked their eyes and ears and took a leap in the dark.

Chris: No, faith is a leap in the light.

Sal: You know, I always thought you believers were softheaded. You sound pretty hardheaded. But soft-hearted.

Chris: Isn't that the right combination? Better than softheaded and hardhearted, isn't it?

Sal: But is your faith based on your head? Are the reasons you're going to give me the real foundation for your life?

Chris: No reasons can be the foundation. You can't base your life on an argument.

Sal: What do you base your life on then?

Chris: God. And my death too.

Sal: But how do you know God, if not by arguments?

Chris: By Jesus. Listening to me argue won't get you as far as reading one of the Gospels and getting to know Jesus.

Sal: Maybe I'm getting to know Jesus a little better just by talking to you. The argument that impresses me already is what your faith seems to do for you. You seem to have a peace and a certainty and a kind of happiness that I just don't have.

Chris: That's more than an argument. And more than me. That's Jesus.

Sal: And that's too heavy for me to handle right now.

Chris: Not Jesus. He's not heavy. He said, "My yoke is easy and my burden is light." And it is.

Sal: Well—we'll see.

Chris: Yes, we will.

Dialogue Two

Faith and Reason

Sal: Chris, before we go any further in our conversations about Christianity, I have to ask you a very basic question.

Chris: Ask away.

Sal: Do you think this is going to get us anywhere, arguing about religion?

Chris: What do you mean by "arguing"?   *Arguing*

Sal: Fighting with words.

Chris: I don't want to do that. We're friends, not enemies. What I mean by "arguing" is just "giving reasons".

Sal: Trying to prove something, right?

Chris: Yes.

Sal: Well, I'm not sure that's going to get us anywhere either.

Chris: Neither am I, but I'm not sure it *isn't*, either. So if there's a chance, let's take it. Let's try.

Sal: Why?

Chris: If a lot of people say a great prize is behind a door, should you try to open it, or not?

Sal: You should, but what does that have to do with arguing?

Chris: The prize here is the truth about God and the meaning of our lives, whatever that truth may be. That's what we're both committed to, isn't it?

Sal: Truth, yes.

Chris: And isn't that valuable, like a prize?

Sal: Yes, if we ever find it.

Chris: Shouldn't we try? Shouldn't we knock at the door?

Sal: What's the door?

Reasons to believe *Chris:* Honest dialogue. Looking for reasons.

Sal: Reasons to believe?

Chris: Yes. Or not to believe.

Sal: I don't think it'll work. I don't think you can reason your way into religion.

Chris: Oh, neither do I. But you might reason your way to the place where you *can* believe—like walking to the beach, and then swimming. Walking to the beach is like reason and swimming is like faith. You have to go to the place where you can swim before you can swim. And you have to go to the place where you can believe before you can believe.

Sal: You mean you have to prove it first by reason before you can believe it?

Chris: No, not at all. But I think it's your reason that's holding you back from believing. I think your reason is asking some good questions that no one has ever answered for you.

Sal: That's true.

Chris: So if we can find the answers to those questions, we can at least make faith *possible* for you. Then it's up to you, of course.

Sal: I see. You agree, then, that religious faith is a matter of personal choice.

Chris: Of course.

Sal: But reason and logic isn't the way we usually make personal choices. Therefore it's not the way to make the choice about religious faith.

Chris: That sounds like pretty good logic, Sal. Let's examine your argument. What do you mean by a "personal choice"?

Sal: What's right for one person can be wrong for another.

Personal choice

Chris: I see. You mean things like getting married or not, or deciding on a career, or how to spend money.

Sal: Right. There's no one right way for everybody.

Chris: But religion isn't like those things, Sal.

Sal: I thought you agreed it was a personal decision.

Chris: I did. But it claims to tell you something that's true for everybody. What's personal is your response to it.

Sal: What do you mean, "true for everybody"? What religious things are true for everybody?

Chris: Things like God and Heaven—whether they're true or not doesn't depend on you, or on your personal choice, any more than the sun does.

Sal: But if I believe it's true, then it's true for me, and if I don't then it isn't true for me.

Chris: Do you think that believing something *makes* it true?

Sal: True for me, yes.

Chris: But *really* true? Objectively true?

Sal: There's no objective truth. Truth is subjective.

Objective truth

Chris: Really?

Sal: Yes.

Chris: Truly?

Sal: Yes.

Chris: I don't think so. Am I wrong? Is this a truth I don't see?

Sal: Yes.

Chris: An objective truth, then. It's an objective truth that there is no objective truth.

Sal: Ooops.

Chris: And you were so logical a minute ago!

Religious truth   **Sal:** Wait a minute. We're talking about *religious* truth. That's subjective.

Chris: You mean nobody can be right or wrong about religious truth?

Sal: Right.

Chris: Except you?

Sal: What do you mean?

Chris: You first said nobody can be right or wrong about religious truth. Then you assumed *you* were right about religious truth when you said it isn't objective.

Sal: You're tangling me up in my words.

Chris: No I'm not. You said it yourself. You tangled yourself up. You contradicted yourself.

Sal: Well, what I mean to say is that nobody can prove whether there really is a God or not.

Chris: Oh, but that's a different question, whether anybody can *prove* it. Surely God might *exist* without your *proving* it. Plenty of things exist that you can't prove, don't they?

Sal: Like what?

Chris: Like the fact that I'm thinking about the color yellow now. Or the fact that I honestly care about you. Can you *prove* those things?

Sal: No.

Chris: Then things can be true without our proving them.

Sal: Yes.

Chris: So God might be true even if we couldn't prove him.

Sal: O.K., but we *can't* prove him. No one can settle religious questions. So I think it's a waste of time to argue about them.

Chris: I see. And why do you think no one can settle religious questions?

Sal: I just think so, that's all.

Chris: You have no reasons to think that?

Sal: Sure I do.

Chris: I think you can guess what my next question is going to be.

Sal: You mean, what are my reasons?

Chris: Good guess.

Sal: Well, you can't prove God like you can prove other things, like galaxies and germs and scientific stuff.

Chris: You mean you can't use the scientific method on God.

Using the scientific method on God

Sal: Right.

Chris: And you think the scientific method is the only way to prove anything.

Sal: *Really* to prove anything, yes.

Chris: Can you prove *that*?

Sal: What?

Chris: What you just said: that the scientific method is the only way to prove anything.

Sal: Hmmm. I guess not.

Chris: Then you contradict yourself again. You say you should believe something only if it's proved scientifically, yet you believe *that* even though it isn't proved scientifically.

Sal: Pretty clever.

Chris: No. I'm not trying to be clever. I'm trying to show you that your faith in science isn't scientific. It's a faith.

Sal: Let me ask the questions for a minute.

Chris: All right.

Sal: Do you think there are other ways to prove things besides the scientific method?

Chris: Yes.

Sal: And can you guess what *my* next question is going to be?

Chris: "What are they?"

Sal: Yes. What are they?

Chris: Common sense, experience, intuition, insight, reasoning, and trustable authority. We use everything we have to look at all the evidence.

Sal: And how do you know which of those methods to use?

Chris: You use the method that fits your subject matter. You don't use the scientific method to understand people you love, for instance, any more than you use love to understand math or chemistry.

Sal: What do you use for God?

Chris: He's a person, so you use the method that fits persons: love and faith.

Sal: That's naïve. Unscientific.

Chris: But it's right for persons. Look. Science is rightly critical and distrustful. It accepts nothing until it's proved. Nature treated as guilty until proven innocent, so to speak. But people are innocent until proven guilty. If we treated people the way science treats nature, we'd never understand them. The only way to understand them is to trust them, not to distrust them. And to love them.

Sal: Just shut your eyes and believe, eh?

Chris: No. Open your eyes and believe.

Sal: But "love is blind."

Love not *blind* *Chris:* Not real love. Real love sees the other person's inside, like an X-ray.

Sal: But sometimes it makes mistakes. Sometimes you trust somebody and he lets you down. Trust doesn't always pay.

Chris: But it's a chance worth taking, isn't it? To live without loving anyone, without trusting anyone—that would be Hell, wouldn't it?

Sal: Yes.

Chris: Worse than being let down, wouldn't it?

Sal: I guess so.

Chris: Well, it's the same with God. It would be even worse never to try him, never to trust him at all, never to give him a chance, than to trust him and then be let down. But he won't let you down.

Sal: So *you* say.

Chris: I'm not asking you to believe it because I say it. I'm asking you to test it, like a good scientist. Faith is like an experiment. It's testable, like trusting a human being. Life is like a laboratory, and loving someone— whether a human being or God—is like an experiment. It's something you do, and you learn by doing.

Sal: I see. It either works or not.

Chris: Yes.

Sal: But I have to have reasons for doing this experiment of believing in God because you're asking me to put *myself* in the test tube. It's not a light little thing.

Chris: I'm glad you see that. It's not a little thing at all. All right, let's look at some reasons for believing in God next time.

Sal: O.K.

Dialogue Three

Can You Prove
That God Exists?

Sal: I hope you're ready, Chris, because today's the day you promised to answer my big question.

Chris: All your questions are big to me, Sal. I take them seriously.

Sal: Thanks for that, by the way. You know, I don't think we could have really good conversations if you weren't a good listener as well as a good talker.

Chris: I'm listening now. What's the question?

Sal: Prove to me that there's a God.

Chris: This isn't just a game to you, is it?

Sal: No. I don't know what to believe. And I want to know.

Chris: What *do* you know?

Sal: Why do you ask that?

Chris: So we can start from there.

Sal: Well, I don't know whether God exists, but I know the world exists, I don't know if religion is true, but I know science is true.

Chris: Fine. Now we have a starting point.

Sal: But how can you bring me from science to God? There's no scientific proof of God.

There is no science without God.

Chris: This way: without God there could be no science.

Sal: What? How do you figure that?

Chris: If there were no universe for science to know, there could be no science, right?

Sal: Of course.

Chris: And if there were no God to create the universe, there could be no universe. Therefore if there were no God, there could be no science.

Sal: I see your argument, but I disagree. I'm free to disagree, after all.

Chris: Yes, and I'm free to ask you why you disagree. I gave you my reason; now you give me yours.

Sal: Fair enough. Well, I don't believe God created the universe.

Chris: Who did then? Walt Disney?

Sal: Nobody. It was always here. You say God always was, right?

Chris: Right.

Sal: Well, why can't I say the universe always was?

Chris: A fair question.

Sal: And have you got a fair answer?

Chris: I think so. I think if you look at this universe you'll find good evidence for a God who made it.

Sal: Where? I don't see it.

Looking with your eyes and not your mind

Chris: Maybe that's because you're looking only with your eyes, not your mind.

Sal: What do you mean by that?

Chris: Maybe you're not asking enough questions.

Sal: Me? I question everything.

Five clues to God

Chris: Then question the universe. Ask it how it got there. If you do, you'll find at least five different clues that point to God. There are many more arguments for God than these five; there are clues all over life, signs that point to God. But these five are based on what you see in nature.

Sal: Sounds solid and scientific so far. Were they invented by some modern scientist?

Chris: No, by a medieval philosopher, Saint Thomas Aquinas.

Sal: Oh.

Chris: You sound disappointed.

Sal: The Middle Ages were primitive.

Chris: In technology, yes. But not in philosophy or theology. Their machines weren't sophisticated, but their minds certainly were.

Sal: Well, what are his five proofs?

Chris: The first one is called the argument from motion. If you see some dominoes in a long row falling down, you know someone pushed them, right?

The argument from motion

Sal: Right.

Chris: Why? How do you know that? Why couldn't they just move themselves?

Sal: Nothing moves itself.

Chris: Right. And neither does the whole universe. Think of the universe as an enormous chain of dominoes, all moving. Something outside the chain must have started the movement in the beginning. Otherwise it couldn't move, because nothing can move itself.

Sal: Wait a minute: we do. We move ourselves.

Chris: Our minds move our bodies, but our bodies don't move themselves. Ever see a corpse move itself? A corpse is just a body without a mind or soul.

Sal: So nothing moves itself.

Chris: And the universe is moving, changing—everything in it is in one great process of change. Therefore . . .

Sal: Therefore there must a first mover. But it's not *God*.

Chris: What is it, then?

Sal: Scientific laws.

Chris: Laws are just descriptions of how things move. You need a real thing, not just a law, really to move another real thing.

Sal: Well, why can't it just be some material thing instead of God?

Chris: All material things make up the whole universe. Part of it can't move all of it. The whole universe needs a mover outside of it, something more than the universe, something supernatural.

Sal: Hmmm. This supernatural something is pretty vague. The God you believe in is much more than that, isn't he?

Chris: Certainly. This argument only proves that there's *some* supernatural cause behind the change in the universe. I know *who* he is from other sources: the Bible and Jesus. But it's the same God. There's only one.

Sal: O.K., what's your second proof?

The argument from existence

Chris: It's the argument from the very existence of things, not just their movement. You need a first cause of existence just as you need a first cause of motion, because nothing can make itself exist if it isn't already there. Nothing can cause itself.

Sal: All right, nothing can cause itself. Nobody can be his own parents. So how does that prove God?

Chris: If there's no God who eternally exists, how can existence begin? If there's no God who *has* existence by his own nature and doesn't get it from any cause, how can the gift of existence be passed down the chain of creatures, who borrow it from each other? If nobody has a certain book, how can others borrow it? If nobody has the authority to give a soldier a weekend pass, how can he ever get it? You can't give what you don't have. So somebody must *have* existence and not just *borrow* it.

Sal: But why couldn't this being that always has existence be a part of the universe? Why does it have to be a God outside the universe, outside of space?

Chris: Outside of *time* too. He has to be eternal, to be uncaused, to have no beginning.

Sal: Why? Kids ask, "If God made everything, who made God?" What do you say to that? Why doesn't God need a cause?

Chris: Because he's first. If nobody's first, nobody can be second, or third, or fourth. But things in the universe *are* second, and third, and fourth, and fifteen-millionth. Therefore there is a first.

Sal: Again, your argument doesn't tell you much about God. Just some thing that's first.

Chris: It tells us that he exists eternally, without beginning, and that he causes the existence of everything else. That's something, at least—enough to bother the atheist, isn't it?

Sal: Yes. What's the third argument?

Chris: It's from observing that everything dies, or ceases to exist. Now if there were no God who never died, who never ceased to exist, then eventually *everything* would die and nothing could begin again. And then there would be nothing at all. But that's absurd. There *is* something.

The argument from death

Sal: Maybe there just hasn't been enough time yet for everything to die, even the stars.

Chris: But if there's no God, no Creator, then there's no beginning to the universe, right?

Sal: Right. The universe always was.

Chris: Well, "always" is enough time for everything. If the universe had no birthday, then there's been an infinity of time already, enough time for everything that could possibly happen to happen. Including the possibility of universal death, universal destruction. So then how come we're still here?

Sal: The universe is only about 15 billion years old. The scientists say the Big Bang happened then.

Chris: And there's another piece of evidence for you. If there's no God, the universe always was. But science itself says the universe came into being 15 billion years ago.

Sal: That's a different argument.

Chris: Yes. The point of this one, Aquinas' third proof, is that without an eternal God everything would eventually cease to be and not be able to create itself anew. Zero, forever.

Sal: Won't that happen? The second law of thermodynamics says all energy gets dissipated, wears down. Even the galaxies get cold, like great big coffee cups.

Chris: The point is, why didn't that happen already if the universe is all there is and has always been there?

Sal: I don't know. Fourth proof, please.

The argument from goodness *Chris:* The fourth one is an easy one. In the universe some things are better than others, right?

Sal: Of course.

Chris: So there must be a best, a standard of goodness to judge all the relative "betters". One thing is closer to it than another. And this standard has to be absolute goodness.

Sal: Why? Everything is relative. There's no absolute.

Chris: Absolutely?

Sal: Oops. Another contradiction. But everything *is* relative.

Chris: To what?

Sal: Not to any absolute. To each other, to everything else. There's just perpetual progress. Nothing is unchanging.

Chris: Progress to what goal? If the goal or standard moves too, how can you ever make progress toward it? How can you steal a moving second base? Progress implies an absolute, unchanging goal or standard.

Sal: So this argument says that if one thing is better than another there has to be a God?

Chris: An absolute good, yes. That's God.

Sal: Well, maybe one thing isn't really better than another. Maybe that's just our way of looking at things.

Chris: You mean maybe people aren't really better than cows?

Sal: Maybe.

Chris: Then why not eat people as well as cows? And why not preach hate as well as love? If goodness is only our prejudice, why pay attention to it?

Sal: You've got me there. I'm not that crazy. Of course love is better than hate, and people are better than cows.

Chris: Then there must be a standard of goodness, a God.

Sal: What's the fifth proof?

Chris: It's the easiest of all. It's called the argument from design. Design proves a designer. And nature is full of design. Therefore there must be a Designer behind it all.

The argument from design

Sal: Can you make that a little less abstract?

Chris: Sure. Suppose you were shipwrecked on a desert island, and you found a message written on the sand in English. Would you think it was written by chance, by the wind?

Sal: Of course not.

Chris: Or if you found a house there, would you think it just evolved by chance?

Sal: No. It would mean there was somebody on the island.

Chris: Well, the universe has more design in it than a house. How could it have happened just by chance? You know, there were two scientists talking to each other as the first moon rocket took off back in the '60s. One was a believer and the other was an atheist. The believer said, "Isn't it wonderful that our rocket is going to hit the moon by chance?" The atheist replied, "What do you mean, by chance? We put billions of hours of planning into that rocket." "Well, if you don't explain the rocket by chance, why do you explain the universe by chance? It's much more complicated than our rocket. We can design a rocket, but we can't design a universe." The same two scientists were walking past an antique store, and the atheist, who was an art collector, saw a painting in the window that attracted him. "Who painted that?" he asked. "Nobody", said the believer. "It just happened by chance."

Sal: It doesn't sound likely, but it just *could* have all happened by chance, you know. If you put a million monkeys at a million typewriters for a million years, they'll eventually type out *Hamlet* just by chance.

Chris: Maybe so. But if you found a copy of *Hamlet*, you wouldn't believe monkeys made it by chance, would you?

Sal: No. It's very improbable. But just possible.

Chris: Why then do you use different standards of explanation when it's a question of God? You don't use the tremendously unlikely explanation for *Hamlet*, or the rocket, or the picture, or the house on the desert island; the only reason you use it for the whole universe is to avoid admitting a God.

Sal: Hmmm. I'm not sure of that. I'll have to reexamine my motives.

Chris: Good. And here's another thing. Would you trust a computer programmed by chance?—by a fall of hailstones on its keyboard, for instance?

Sal: No.

Chris: Or if you were flying in an airplane and the public address system announced that the plane was being flown by a computer that had been programmed by a football player in spiked shoes walking over computer cards, would you trust the airplane to land you safely?

Sal: No way.

Chris: They why do you trust your brain and nervous system? It's like a very complex computer. If it's been programmed only by chance, by blind nature, and not by God, not by any Designer, why trust it when it does science, and when it tells you about nature? Or about itself? If you can't trust the programmer of the human brain, then you can't trust the brain when it tells you about the brain!

Why trust the brain?

Sal: O.K., Chris, they're good arguments. But as I told you, I can't base my life on an argument.

Chris: And as I told you, I don't do that either. But they *are* strong clues, at least—signs, evidence all pointing to God.

Sal: I'll have to admit that much, if I'm honest. But I still don't believe in God.

Chris: You will. Honesty is the beginning of the love of God.

Sal: Why do you say that?

Chris: Because honesty is the love of truth. And God is truth.

Dialogue Four

Science and Religion

Sal: Chris! Look at that beautiful sunset!

Chris: Oh! Thanks, Sal.

Sal: Thanks for the sunset? Who do you think I am, God? I didn't make the sunset.

Chris: No, I mean to thank you for calling my attention to it. And thanks to God for making it. What a pity you have no one to thank when something as beautiful as that is given to you?

Sal: Hmph! I don't need your God; I have science to explain everything. Your religion is a crutch for weak minds. You use superstition; I use science.

Chris: Since when is "beautiful" a scientific term?

Sal: It isn't.

Chris: But you just called the sunset beautiful. You're not being scientific.

Sal: Oh. Sorry. I didn't really mean it.

Chris: You mean the sunset isn't really beautiful?

Sal: Right. It's just a dance of molecules. The beauty isn't really in it. It's in us, in our feelings.

Chris: The beauty is in you, not the sunset?

Sal: Yes.

Chris: But that's silly. You're not that beautiful. The sunset is!

Sal: I mean the beauty is in my feelings, not in my face.

Chris: You *felt* beautiful when you looked at the sunset?

Sal: No. I'm *not* that beautiful. But I feel the sunset is.

Chris: Then according to your feelings, the sunset really is beautiful, there really is beauty out there?

Sal: According to my feelings, yes. But my feelings are wrong. There's no real beauty out there. How can feelings tell you what the real world out there is like?

Chris: Why not? Why can't feelings be just as true as reasoning?

Sal: Oh, come on, now. That's just plain silly.

Chris: You didn't answer my question: Why can't feelings be true?

Sal: I guess I don't know, I just feel it.

Chris: And that feeling—is it true?

Sal: You're tangling me up in my words again.

Chris: No, you're doing it to yourself again.

Sal: But what's the point of talking about feelings? Is that what your faith is? A feeling? Is that what you meant by thanking God for the sunset?

Faith and feelings *Chris:* No, faith is more than feeling. Feeling changes a hundred times a day; faith doesn't. But all three might be ways to know truth: faith, *and* feeling, *and* scientific reasoning. So the sunset might really be a gift of God *and* beautiful *and* dancing molecules.

Sal: Well, no religious dogma for me.

Chris: *That's* a dogma. You exclude religion as a way to know truth, without any proof for your exclusion. That's dogmatic. But I don't exclude your scientific method. I'm not dogmatic. I include you but you don't include me. My religion includes your science, but your science—no, your faith that science alone is true—refuses to include my religion.

Sal: You can be religious all you want. But that's not an explanation of the real world.

Chris: Sure it is. Why not?

Sal: I suppose you think that sunset is half made of molecules and half of gods?

Chris: No, it's made all *of* molecules, but it's all made *by* God. Those are two different questions—one for science and one for religion to answer.

Sal: No. Science answers religion's question too. For instance, the sunset wasn't made by God but by gravity rotating the earth and by refraction of sunlight through the atmosphere. Don't you know that?

Chris: I know it was made by gravity and refraction, but who made gravity and refraction? Who made the sun and the sunlight?

Sal: Rotating galaxies and cooling gas clouds.

Chris: And who made the galaxies and gas clouds?

Sal: It all started with a "Big Bang" 15 billion years ago.

Chris: And who started the Big Bang?

Sal: That's not a scientific question.

Chris: Exactly. And therefore science has no answer to it. But religion does. It's not a scientific question not because it's not about the real world—it *is*—but because science can't answer a question about God, who's outside the universe, just by looking at the inside of the universe.

Sal: The whole universe sort of leans on God, then, like a crutch, according to you, right? And you lean on him too. Well, I don't need a crutch. That's what religion is: a crutch.

Chris: Right.

Sal: What?

Religion is a crutch.

Chris: I said right. I agree. Religion is a crutch.

Sal: Why do you believe it then?

Chris: Because we're all cripples.

Sal: Oh come on!

Chris: I mean it. We're all mentally and emotionally handicapped. That's the great lesson I learned last summer working with handicapped kids: that I'm handicapped too, but in different ways. We all are. You know, they taught me much more than I could teach them.

Sal: Well, I don't think I'm handicapped. I don't need any crutches, for my mind or my emotions. My head and heart are quite well, thank you.

Chris: *My* handicaps include irritability, fear of pain, and impatience. But you have no handicaps, eh? And you're perfectly happy?

Sal: Of course not . . .

Chris: Then you need help. Crutches.

Sal: You can't prove that I need *God*.

Chris: Not if you won't look at your own heart, no.

Sal: What do you mean, my own heart?

Chris: I can only ask you to be honest with your heart. Have you really found happiness without God? Can you be your own God, your own good, your own happiness-giver, your own final end and reason and purpose for living?

Sal: That's really my own private affair, isn't it?

Chris: Yes. And a very serious one.

Sal: Then we can't talk about it objectively.

Chris: No, but we can talk about your head, your reason, your science.

What's missing in science

Sal: All right, why do you think I need God as a crutch for my science? Why does science limp? What's missing? It seems to be doing quite well.

Chris: The First Cause of all is missing. There's the real "Missing Link" in science's explanation of the world: the very first link.

Sal: Science doesn't need a first link. The rest of the chain holds together perfectly without it. Science can explain the world perfectly well without God, even if it can't explain the first cause of it all.

Chris: Well, here's a second thing it can't explain: Why does science work at all?

Sal: Because we have brains, of course.

Chris: And religion explains why our brains work so well: because God designed them.

Sal: Science explains them better: they evolved.

Chris: By chance or by divine design?

Sal: By chance and "natural selection"—trial and error. Over millions of years, the brains that worked survived and those that didn't died out.

Chris: If your brain evolved just by chance, why should I trust it to know the truth?

Sal: That's the argument from design that you used yesterday.

Chris: Have you thought up an answer to it?

Sal: No.

Chris: And here's another problem I mentioned before: you can't prove the scientific method by the scientific method. So if you say you believe *only* what can be proved by the scientific method, you can't prove *that*. So you'd better not believe it.

Sal: I've got an answer to that one, Chris. I believe it because it works.

Chris: But why does it work?

Sal: It just does, that's all.

Chris: You can't explain why?

Sal: I guess not.

Chris: Well, I can.

Sal: God, eh?

Chris: Yep.

Sal: All right, I couldn't answer your three questions, see if you can answer mine. You accept science, don't you?

Chris: Yes.

Sal: So if science discovers something true, then it's really true, right?

Chris: Right.

Sal: And if science says one thing and religion says another, if there's a contradiction between them, then one of the two has to be wrong doesn't it?

Chris: Yes.

Sal: So if science is true and religion contradicts it, then religion is false.

Does religion contradict science? *Chris:* Oh, but religion never does contradict it.

Sal: Never?

Chris: Never. Show me one discovery of science that contradicts one belief of my religion.

Sal: That's easy. Evolution.

Evolution *Chris:* Evolution is a *theory*. I asked for a *discovery*.

Sal: Science has discovered evolution.

Chris: No. Science has discovered a lot of old bones.

Sal: And they prove evolution. Man evolved from the apes.

Chris: No, they prove we came after the apes, if the dating is right. But *how* we came is another question. Science can't see the answer to that question in bones. How could it?

Sal: But nearly all scientists believe the theory of evolution. Don't you?

Chris: I honestly don't know. I'm not a scientist. And neither are you.

Sal: So we have to go by what the real scientists tell us.

Chris: Nearly all scientists once believed the earth was at the center of the universe. But they were wrong. Science is not infallible. It's always correcting itself.

Sal: But they were *medieval* scientists!

Chris: They thought of themselves as modern, the latest thing. And scientists of the year 3,000 will see *us* as "medieval" or "ancient".

Sal: Do you accept the theory of evolution or not?

Chris: I told you, I don't know. But suppose I did. How would that contradict my faith?

Sal: Evolution says we evolved from apes; your faith says we were created by God. Are we made in the image of King Kong or made in the image of King God? That sounds like a contradiction to me.

Chris: But evolution doesn't tell us *who* made us, and the Bible doesn't tell us *how* God made us, except that it says God made Adam "out of the dust of the ground" —out of something, some stuff, some previously existing material. Why couldn't that be an ape's body? Dust, evolving to the human body through bacteria and plants and animals and apes. But *however* our bodies came to be, that's only half the story.

Sal: What do you mean, half the story?

Chris: Science can't see the soul, or tell us how the soul originated.

Science can't explain the soul.

Sal: Maybe there's no such thing as a soul.

Chris: Then there's no such thing as a person, only a machine. Or a corpse. Because that's what a body without a soul is, a corpse. Do you think you're a corpse?

Sal: Of course not.

Chris: Then you have a soul. And the Bible tells us that God put a soul into us. There's no contradiction between our saying our body came from apes and our soul came from God. Or rather that our soul came from God directly and our body indirectly—because apes came from God too. Everything did.

Sal: You may have explained away that contradiction, but I doubt if you can explain away all the other ones.

Chris: What other ones?

Sal: Well . . . don't you think there will *ever* be *any* contradiction between science and religion?

Chris: Certainly not. God doesn't contradict himself.

Sal: God? God doesn't come into science.

Chris: He sure does. He wrote two books, nature and Scripture, and the two books can never contradict each other because they come from the same author, who is Truth itself. Truth can never contradict truth.

Sal: So if I can show you a contradiction between science and Scripture, I've proved my point.

Chris: Yes, and I'm still waiting.

Sal: That's a fair challenge. I'll come back when I find one.

Chris: Oh, please come back before that, or I'll never see you again!

Dialogue Five

The Problem of Evil

Sal: Chris, I've got a real tough one for you today.

Chris: A tough question?

Sal: Yes.

Chris: I don't have *all* the answers, you know.

Sal: Well, I sure hope you have the answer to this one, because it's the best argument against God I've ever seen.

Chris: Oh, the problem of evil?

Sal: How did you know that was the one I meant?

Chris: It's the *only* really tough argument against God. How would you put it?

The only really tough argument against God

Sal: This way. It sounds awfully simple and unanswerable. God is supposed to be completely good, right?

Chris: Right.

Sal: And also completely powerful, right?

Chris: Right.

Sal: And evil things really happen, right?

Chris: Right. Terrible things. Suffering and death and injustice.

Sal: Well, if there's a God running the world with his power, then he must want these bad things to happen, and then he's not good. And if God doesn't want them to happen and they do anyway, then he's not all-powerful.

49

Chris: That's a very strong way of putting the argument.

Sal: I don't want a compliment. I want an answer.

Two questions about evil *Chris:* Let's begin by distinguishing two different questions about evil. The first question is where evil came from. Did God make it? The second question is where it's going to end up. What's God doing about it? Why doesn't he destroy it all right now?

Sal: Now you've got *two* questions to answer instead of one. You're making it harder for yourself.

Chris: No, I'm just trying to get rid of confusion so that I can answer the two questions in different ways.

Where does evil come from? *Sal:* Well, let's hear your answer to the first one. Didn't God make everything?

Chris: Yes.

Sal: Then he must have made evil too. How can a good God make evil?

Chris: He didn't make evil.

Sal: But you just said he made everything.

Chris: Yes. Evil's not a thing. He made every *thing*.

Sal: You mean evil isn't real?

Chris: Of course it's real. I didn't say that. I said it's not a *thing*.

Sal: What is it, then?

Chris: Look here: If I hit you with a rock, that's evil, right?

Sal: I'll say.

Chris: But the *rock* isn't evil, is it?

Sal: No. In fact you have to find a *good* rock to hit me with.

Chris: Well, is my hand evil?

Sal: No. You have two good hands.

Chris: So what *is* evil? The choice to hit you is evil. The act of hitting you is evil.

Sal: That's right.

Chris: Well, God didn't make that choice or that act. I did.

Sal: I thought God made everything.

Chris: Every *thing*, yes. Every rock and hand and fish and star and atom and angel, yes. But he didn't make my choices or my acts. I make them with my own free will. If I choose evil, I'm to blame, not God.

Sal: But he created you.

Chris: Yes, but he created me good. I'm not evil until I choose to do an evil act.

Sal: But God gave you the power to do evil acts and the power freely to choose evil in your will.

Chris: Yes, but power isn't evil by itself. Only using it in the wrong way is evil. The power in my arm is good. God gave it to me, and he wants me to use it for good. If I use it for evil, that's not God. The power in my will to choose is good too, and God gave me that. But I can use it wrongly, against God's will.

Sal: All right, but why does God *allow* you to do evil? Why does he allow terrible evils? Why did he allow Hitler to kill six million Jews and other people? Couldn't he perform a miracle and stop it, if he's all-powerful?

Chris: All right, now you're asking the second question: not where evil comes from but where it's going to, what God is doing about it. Are you satisfied with my answer to the first question, before we go on to the second?

What is God doing about evil?

Sal: Yes. Evil comes from our free choice. But why did God give us free choice in the first place?

Chris: Because he loved human beings, not robots or puppets.

Sal: All right, but why doesn't he zap all the bad guys now, and heal all the sick people?

Chris: I think it's the same reason our parents don't do our homework for us.

Sal: What do you mean?

Chris: You tell me. Why don't parents do homework for their children?

Sal: I know the answer to that one. If they did, their children wouldn't learn anything.

Chris: And that wouldn't be good for students, would it?

Sal: No.

Chris: But doing homework sometimes is a pain, isn't it?

Sal: Yes.

Chris: And parents could take that pain away if they gave their children the answers, couldn't they?

Sal: Yes.

Chris: Are parents evil because they don't take that pain away?

Sal: Of course not. They're good.

Chris: Even though they let their children suffer?

Sal: Yes.

Chris: So just because someone lets you suffer, that doesn't necessarily mean that person is evil.

Sal: No.

Chris: So even though God lets us suffer sometimes, that doesn't mean he's evil either.

Sal: Oh. But the sufferings in the world are a lot worse than homework!

Chris: Of course. I just wanted to show you that someone who is good and loves you could still let you suffer sometimes.

Sal: But why does God let so *much* of it go on? A lot of it is terrible suffering. And why does he let good people suffer as much as bad people?

Chris: Those are very hard questions, and I'm afraid I don't know the answer to them.

Sal: Oh.

A complete answer is unknown.

Chris: I'm sorry to disappoint you, but I told you before that I don't have all the answers. I'll tell you what I know and I'll tell you what I don't know. No faking it.

Sal: Thanks for being honest, anyway. But how can you still believe in a good God if you don't know why he lets people suffer?

Chris: I know *why* he lets people suffer, I just don't know how he figures it all out. He lets people suffer for the same reason he does everything: he loves us.

Sal: How is it love when he lets a young child die of cancer?

Chris: I don't know. If I knew all the answers to questions like that, I wouldn't have to believe him. He asks us to trust him, even when we don't understand.

Sal: I don't understand how you can take such a passive attitude. Just trust God no matter what?

Chris: Oh, we don't take a passive attitude toward evil. We fight it, in ourselves and in the world (though the weapons we use aren't guns). The most important question about evil is not where it came from but what to do about it, and the answer is to fight it. That's not passive. That's active.

Sal: But where is God in this?

Chris: He didn't originate evil, and he's fighting against it with us, *in* us, even. We're fighting for him when we fight disease, or prejudice, or tyranny.

God fights evil.

Sal: All right, you've kept God *good*, but if he has to fight evil he can't be all-powerful.

Chris: I know for sure that God is all good. I also see that—in Jesus. I believe God is also all-powerful. But I don't see that power, even in Jesus. He died too, and that didn't look like power. But he also rose from the dead, and that was a kind of sign and a promise that God can do anything and that he will conquer all evil in the end.

Sal: Meanwhile, here we are up to our necks in it. Why doesn't he just clean up all the evil now?

Chris: Because he wants *us* to do it. That's part of growing up: doing things for yourself. He's a good Father; he doesn't do everything for his children, even though he can.

Sal: Do you believe he will wipe out all evil in the end?

Chris: Yes. He has told us that. It's in the Bible.

Sal: Why does he wait? Why can't we be at the end now?

Chris: We're in time, like being somewhere in a story that takes time to get to the end. You're asking why we're in the middle of the story now and not at the end. But you have to go through the middle to get to the end, just because it's a story. Every story takes time. You're asking God to create a world without time, a story that gets to the end right away.

Sal: I still feel resentment and hate when I see terribly unjust things happen. I want to blame God even though I don't believe in God.

Chris: But if you blame God, you blame our only hope for conquering evil in the end. He's on our side. He hates evil too. The Bible is full of that. That's why he's so insistent about his laws.

Sal: I think you're just leaping in the dark when you believe in a good God who's going to conquer all evil in the end. That sounds too good to be true. I want to see more evidence before I make that leap. It's hard to trust a God who lets his world get so bad.

Chris: I agree.

Sal: What? I thought you were such a strong believer.

Chris: I do believe. But you're right that it's hard to trust God sometimes, when things go very wrong. It's like a dog trusting a hunter who's trying to get him out of a bear trap; the only way the hunter can do that is to push the dog *into* the trap farther first, and that doesn't look like something good. It also hurts. But it's really the best thing for the dog. He can't see that. He just has to trust the hunter.

Trusting God when things go wrong

Sal: That's a nice analogy, but it's not like that with us and God. We don't see any hunter getting us out of the trap of evil.

Chris: Yes we do: Jesus Christ. He came right down into our trap and died to free us. The One who asks us to trust him to solve the problem of evil already did the greatest thing to conquer it. He suffered every kind of evil with us. He was hated by the people he loved. He was nailed to a cross, and died. He even felt his Father leave him horribly alone on the cross, when he said, "My God, my God, why have you forsaken me?" *That's* evil. All the evil in the world is there, and there he is in the middle of it. You think of God up in Heaven controlling things down here and you wonder why he doesn't do a better job. You wonder if he really cares, and how he can be good if he just stays there and turns away and lets terrible things happen. But it's not like that. He didn't stay away. He came down into evil. That's the Christian answer to the problem of evil: not a tricky argument, but Christ on the cross, God on our side, the side of the innocent sufferer. How can you resent a God like *that*?

Sal: I was thinking of the faraway God.

Chris: It *would* be hard to trust a God like that. No, that's not our God. If you want to know what our God is like, look at Jesus.

Sal: Now that's a whole new question. I can certainly

love and admire Jesus. But Jesus was a man. How can a man be God?

Chris: You have a great way of asking all the good questions. Let's look at that one tomorrow.

Sal: It's a date.

Dialogue Six

Who Is Jesus?

Sal: Chris, you surprised me with your answer to the problem of evil yesterday. You didn't answer with God the Father in Heaven but with God the Son, Jesus, suffering evil on the cross. That makes God much more lovable—*if* that's God on the cross. That's the big question.

Chris: Yes it is.

Sal: If Jesus is just another good man who suffered unjustly, then he makes the problem of evil worse rather than solving it.

Chris: You're absolutely right, Sal. You see the connection very clearly. A Jewish friend of mine once asked me, "Where was God during the holocaust, when six million Jews were put into gas ovens?" I said that God was in the gas ovens. Jesus was Jewish too, you know. But the point is that he suffered not only his own pains but ours too. But he can't do that if he was only a man, and not God.

Sal: So your answer doesn't work except for Christians.

Chris: That's right. Christianity is a package deal. It all hangs together. It's not like a supermarket, where you can pick some products and leave others, or like a smorgasbord, but like a meal at home where your mother says, "Eat everything on your plate."

How could a man be God?

Sal: Well, I just can't believe a man was God. Did Jesus get dirt under his fingernails?

Chris: He sure did.

Sal: How could that be God? That's just crazy.

Chris: I'm glad you see how amazing it is. Most Christians don't appreciate that. They just take it for granted.

Sal: You don't blame me for questioning it, then?

Chris: I'm always glad to see you asking honest questions.

Sal: Aren't you afraid someone with weak faith will read this and lose his faith?

Chris: Yes, I am; I don't want to help anyone lose his faith, because faith is a precious thing, a jewel. But if anyone's faith is so weak that he loses it just because someone points out how amazing Jesus' claim is, or just because someone says it's O.K. to ask honest questions, then I think *that* faith *should* be lost, *has* to be lost. It wasn't that precious jewel I was talking about. I've known some people who found real faith in Christ only after losing their old weak faith. It's like tearing down a weak old building to build another, stronger one.

Sal: So the important thing is how *strong* your faith is?

Chris: No, how *honest* it is. The one thing everyone must start with is total honesty, I think. To believe just because it's easier, or convenient—or to refuse to believe just because it's easy or convenient—that's not honest.

Convenience vs. honesty

Sal: What do you mean, convenient? What could make believing convenient or inconvenient? Give me an example.

Chris: If I decide to stop believing just so that I can commit all the sins I want without feeling guilty, without asking what's true and what God thinks—that's dishonest. And to decide to believe just to avoid the hassle of thinking for myself or just because it's socially convenient—that's dishonest too.

Sal: Can't someone believe other parts of Christianity but not this part—that Christ is God?

Chris: No. Christ is like the front door of the house. Through it, through him, you enter all the other rooms.

Christ the door

Sal: I don't follow your figure of speech.

Chris: If Christ is God, then everything he teaches is true. And all the things Christians believe, they believe because he taught them.

Sal: I thought you Christians had to believe thousands of things—all sorts of doctrines and creeds and laws and commandments.

Chris: Ultimately, just one thing: Christ. Everything else is because of him. Christians differ a bit on what things can be traced to him—Catholics say the teachings of the Church, Protestants say just what's in the Bible—but we all believe his teachings ultimately because we believe him. The object of our Faith is not a thousand things but one Person.

Sal: I thought you believed those thousand things because your Church taught them.

Chris: Not *my* church; his Church.

Sal: But she does teach a thousand things.

Chris: Maybe. I never counted. But I'd believe a billion things if he said so.

Sal: Because you believe he was God.

Chris: *Is* God. He's alive. He rose from the dead.

Sal: We have to talk about that some day too. But I think you believe only because you've been conditioned to believe, by your parents and teachers and Church.

Conditioning vs. teaching *Chris:* Not *conditioned*, like a rat in a maze. I've been *taught*, like a free human being in a conversation, like the one we're having now. I'm able to disbelieve; I choose to believe.

Sal: Taught, then. But you only believe because you've been taught. If you had never heard about Christianity, you wouldn't believe it.

Chris: Of course not. And if you hadn't heard about the planet Pluto, you wouldn't believe it either. That doesn't mean it isn't true, or that you believe it *only* because your teachers say so.

Sal: Didn't you learn Christianity from teachers?

Chris: Of course. Everyone does, except Christ himself. My teachers passed on to me what they learned from their teachers, who eventually go back to Jesus' first disciples and to Jesus himself.

Sal: Don't stories get garbled when they're handed down through the generations?

God's newspaper *Chris:* That's why Jesus' disciples wrote the Gospels. There's the story, in God's newspaper.

Sal: Well, why do you believe *that* story?

Chris: For the same reason Jesus' first disciples did, the same reason Christians through the centuries believed: because I've met him.

Sal: You had a mystical experience?

Chris: No, I met him in the Gospels and in his disciples.

Sal: That's too personal to argue about. Can you put it into an argument?

Chris: Yes, but the argument isn't the object of my faith: he is.

Sal: O.K. But what's the argument?

Chris: You need data first, to argue about. You get that from the Gospels. Read them. Imagine you were

Peter, or John, or one of the Marys, or any one of Jesus' friends. You get to know Jesus. You live with him. You hear him teach. You see him heal.

Sal: I've read the Gospels.

Chris: Who do you say Jesus is, then?

Who is Jesus?

Sal: A good man, a wise man, a great moral teacher.

Chris: Not a bad man?

Sal: Of course not. Nobody thinks he's a bad man.

Chris: An awful lot of people did 2,000 years ago. They got him killed because they thought he was a bad man—a very, very bad man.

Sal: How could anyone think that?

Chris: Easy. He claimed to be God. If he *isn't* God, as you say he isn't, then he isn't a good man but a blasphemer or an idiot: a very bad man.

Sal: Hmmm.

Chris: Did I go too fast with the argument?

Sal: Yes. Let's back up and gather the data.

Chris: Good. The data is two things: one, he is a good, loving, wise, generous, trustable man. And clever—he had terrific insight into people. A cool head and a warm heart. That's the picture you get from the Gospels, isn't it?

Sal: Yes. What's the second thing?

Chris: That he claimed to be God. "Before Abraham was, I Am." "I am the Resurrection and the life. He who believes in me will never die." "I am the way, the truth, and the life; no one can come to the Father except through me." He forgives sins . . .

Sal: Wait a minute. Aren't we supposed to forgive sins too?

Forgiveness of sins

Chris: Sins against us, yes. But he forgave *all* sins. Can you do that?

Sal: Why not?

Chris: If you stole your sister's money, could I forgive you for that?

Sal: No. *She* has to forgive me.

Chris: So only the one offended has the right to forgive.

Sal: Yes.

Chris: And he forgave all sins. That implies that he is the one offended in all sins. And who is that?

Sal: God. I see. But just because he *claimed* to be God doesn't mean he *was*. People claim all sorts of crazy things.

Chris: Crazy people, yes. Dishonest people, yes. Stupid people, yes. Which do you think he was?

Sal: A good man.

Chris: That's the one and only thing he couldn't possibly be.

Sal: Why?

Lord, liar, or lunatic

Chris: Because if he isn't God, then he's either a liar or a lunatic to claim to be God. A liar if he knew he wasn't God, a lunatic if he thought he was. What is he: Lord, liar, or lunatic?

Sal: A prophet, maybe.

Chris: Would you call me a prophet if I said I was God?

Sal: Of course not. I'd call you nuts.

Chris: Then why do you call Jesus a prophet? None of the prophets claimed to be God. If Jesus' claim is true, he's much more than a prophet: he's God. And if it isn't true, then he's much less than a prophet: he's a false prophet; a blasphemer, a liar, or a lunatic.

Sal: That's a clever argument.

Chris: I don't want compliments.

Sal: What do you want?

Chris: Honesty. Be honest with yourself. Dare to ask the question: Who is Jesus, really?

Sal: I can't answer your argument.

Chris: It's Jesus, not the argument, that's important. The argument is only an arrow, pointing to him. Who is he? There's your puzzle, your challenge, if you dare to face up to it. I know you're too honest just to look the other way, Sal. You have to do something with him. Here's the man who claims to be your Lord and your God and your Savior. If he is, you'd better believe in him. If he's not, you'd better not call him a good man, but a bad man.

Sal: There's got to be a way out of that.

Chris: Why? Why are you looking for a way out? What are you afraid of?

Sal: Another hard question. I don't know.

Chris: Are you going to avoid that question too? The first question was about Christ, and you tried to avoid that by looking for a way out. The second question was about you: What's motivating you to run away from Christ's claim on you? Are you going to face those two questions or run away from them?

Sal: Chris, stop badgering me!

Chris: I'm just asking you to be honest with yourself.

Sal: O.K., I'll face the question. Maybe the way out is that the Bible just isn't true—maybe Jesus never existed, or maybe he was completely different from what the Bible says. Maybe he never claimed to be God. Prove to me that the Bible is true.

Chris: Gladly—some other day. But not to find a way out of today's question.

Sal: I do really want to know. I want a way *in*, not a way out: a way to find out what's true.

Chris: Then I know you'll find it.

Sal: How do you know that?

Chris: Because Jesus promised it: "Seek and you shall find; all who seek find."

Seek and you shall find.

Sal: And you believe that.

Chris: Yes.

Sal: Because he's God.

Chris: Yes. It all hangs together.

Sal: So how do I know what's true?

Chris: There's only one way to find out.

Sal: Just believe, you mean?

Chris: No, seek. It's the same as in the sciences. If you don't ask questions, if you don't examine your data, you'll never find answers. And here the data is Jesus.

Sal: How do I look at Jesus more deeply? I've read the Gospels.

Chris: Do you really want to look more deeply?

Sal: In an open-minded way, yes.

Chris: Then read them again, more searchingly. And here's a second thing to do that I'll bet you've not done.

Sal: What?

Chris: Pray.

Sal: How can I pray if I don't believe? That's dishonest.

The seeker's prayer   *Chris:* No. Just be honest. Say something like this: "Jesus, I'm not sure whether you're God or not. If you're only a good man who's dead, you can't even hear me. But if you're God, you must want me to know that, to know you, to believe in you. I just want to know the truth. Please show me the truth." If you honestly mean that prayer, you'll find him. He promised that. The prayer is a kind of experiment, a test. But you really have to mean it; you really have to seek. The promise was that only seekers find.

Sal: I like that. It's almost scientific. Do you think I'll see some miracle?

Chris: No, he didn't promise *how* we'd find him.

Sal: How long do you think it will take?

Chris: I don't know. He didn't promise *when* we'd find him either. But he did promise the most important thing: that we'd find him.

Sal: I'll do it.

Dialogue Seven

The Resurrection

Sal: Chris, I've been thinking about this Jesus you worship, and about your argument last time.

Chris: In that order, I hope. First things first.

Sal: Yes. Here's how I see it. If I should ever decide to believe this guy is God, then that's got to change my whole life, not just get tucked away in a corner of my mind to be remembered on Sunday mornings in church. Isn't that right?

Chris: It certainly is.

Sal: That's why I can't decide to believe just because I can't answer your argument. I can't stake my life on an argument. That would be like building a skyscraper on a dime. Do you understand why I'm hesitating?

Chris: I understand perfectly, Sal.

Sal: I can't base my whole life on just one belief. I have to base my life on facts.

Facts, faith, feelings

Chris: So do I.

Sal: I thought you built your life on faith.

Chris: But faith has to be based on facts.

Sal: Not feelings?

Chris: Certainly not.

Sal: Are you against feelings?

Chris: No. They come along too, like the caboose pulled by the train. Faith is like the train, and feelings are like the caboose, but fact is like the locomotive.

Sal: The early Christians didn't think that way, did they?

Chris: They certainly did.

Sal: But they weren't scientific.

Chris: We can know facts in other ways besides science, you know.

Sal: How?

Chris: We use our senses, and experience the facts ourselves. And we get to know trustworthy people who tell us what *they* saw or experienced and we believe it if we believe them.

Sal: You mean like firsthand accounts and secondhand accounts? Like eyewitnesses to an accident and reading the report in the newspaper?

Chris: Exactly. And that's how the early Christians knew the facts about Jesus: his disciples experienced him firsthand, and they told others. Church and Bible are mail carriers and mail.

Sal: Chris, you say Christianity is based on facts. Isn't it mainly about values? Love and all that? Isn't Christianity the religion of love?

Chris: Of course Christianity is the religion of love. But the Gospel, the "good news", the Christian message, the headline in God's newspaper, the thing that turned the world upside down—this wasn't "love one another". The Jews had known that for many centuries, ever since Moses.

Sal: What's new then?

The Resurrection   *Chris:* That the God of love who became a man— Jesus—had risen from the dead. *That's* the fact we base our faith on.

Sal: I see. If it really happened, it proves he's God. Because it takes God to conquer death, not just a good man.

Chris: Yes.

Sal: But did it really happen? That's the question.

Chris: That *is* the question.

Sal: Couldn't it be a myth? Couldn't you believe the rest of Christianity without believing in the Resurrection?

A lovely myth?

Chris: Nope. Look. Here's what Saint Paul says in 1 Corinthians 15: "If Christ has not been raised, then our preaching is in vain and your faith is in vain. . . . If Christ has not been raised, your faith is futile and you are still in your sins."

Sal: Isn't it enough to have Christ as a model for this life?

Chris: Not according to his disciples. Look what Saint Paul says next: "If for this life only we have hoped in Christ, we are of all men most to be pitied."

Sal: Wow! That's pretty clear. But I heard a religion teacher say the opposite the other day, in class.

Chris: Who's closer to Jesus, Saint Paul or your religion teacher?

Sal: But he's a clergyman!

Chris: So?

Sal: Can't you trust the clergy?

Chris: Not if they don't trust the Bible!

Sal: But it seems so reasonable to believe the Resurrection is just a lovely myth, like the Easter Bunny. Why couldn't the disciples have just made up the story that Jesus rose from the dead to give the people something to believe in? Doesn't that seem more reasonable?

Chris: No.

Sal: Why not?

Chris: First of all, if there's a God who created this whole universe out of nothing, he can certainly raise one man's body from the dead, can't he? If he can do one miracle, he can do another.

Sal: That's reasonable, yes.

Chris: Second, if Jesus didn't really rise from the dead, then his disciples were liars. They kept preaching that he had risen and that they had seen him and talked with him and touched him.

Sal: Maybe they weren't liars, just mistaken. Maybe they had a hallucination.

Chris: All of them? The same hallucination?

Sal: Could be.

Chris: Read the accounts in the four Gospels and the first chapter of Acts. It's not at all like a dream or a hallucination. He spends forty days with them. Forty days!—a pretty long hallucination. They touch his wounds. He eats with them, to prove he's not a ghost.

Sal: O.K., so it's not a hallucination. It's a myth, a story. The disciples weren't deceived, they were deceivers. Isn't that more reasonable than a literal Resurrection? Isn't it more likely that a bunch of men tell a lie, than a man rises from the grave?

Chris: No, it isn't. Work it out. Think it through. What did they get out of their lie? Persecuted, tortured, imprisoned, exiled, jeered at, and killed, that's what. Now why would anyone live and suffer and die for a lie if he knew it was a lie? People are fickle and changeable; under torture they surely would have confessed that it was all a lie, and then the whole thing would have stopped. The cat would be out of the bag. But that didn't happen. What kept them going after Jesus left them? A lie?

Sal: That doesn't seem right.

Chris: And here's another thing. This "lie" has helped millions of people to live and die, has given deep meaning and purpose and joy and hope to millions of lives for 2,000 years. Can a lie do that?

Sal: Santa Claus does it for little kids.

Chris: Only one day a year. This does it for the other 364. And for grownups. The greatest mental grownups, the wisest minds in history have believed: Augustine, Aquinas, Newton, Pascal, Kierkegaard, C. S. Lewis—the list is endless.

Sal: I wish I could talk to a scientific historian about the Resurrection. I'm sure he could explain it away.

Chris: There was such a man once. His name was Frank Morrison. He thought Christianity was a superstition and he set out to prove to the world that Jesus didn't really rise from the dead. He used all the most scientific tools of historical research to explain away the evidence.

History and the Resurrection

Sal: Sounds like I'd like his book. What evidence?

Chris: All the evidence: the disciples' claim, the empty tomb, the rock rolled away, the authorities not being able to produce Jesus' dead body—that would have ended the whole thing, right then.

Sal: Maybe the disciples stole it.

Chris: That's what he thought. He tried to prove that, and the more he looked at the evidence scientifically and rationally, the more he became convinced that there was only one possible rational explanation, if he was to use the same standards for this as for other historical evidence.

Sal: What?

Chris: That Jesus did rise from the dead. So the book he had planned to write *against* the Resurrection became a book *for* it. It's called *Who Moved the Stone?*

Sal: I'd like to read it. But if you don't believe in miracles, you have to rule that explanation out from the beginning, don't you?

Chris: You can't just make up your mind not to believe in miracles without any reasons, without evidence. That's prejudice, not reason. You have to look at the evidence first. And if the evidence shows that Jesus really did rise from the dead—if *this* miracle happened—why, then miracles *do* happen.

Sal: *If* miracles can happen, then the Resurrection can happen. But if miracles can't happen, then the Resurrection couldn't have happened either, no matter how hard it is to explain the disciples' faith without a real Resurrection. I don't know whether they were liars or hallucinating, but either of those two theories seems more likely than a miracle.

Chris: Only if you begin by assuming that miracles never happen.

Sal: Well, let's talk about that next. It all hangs together.

Chris: Yes.

Dialogue Eight

Miracles

Sal: You know, Chris, I'm really impressed by how everything you believe is tied together. I can't believe all the things Jesus said, as you do, because I can't believe Jesus was God. And I can't believe Jesus was God because I can't believe he rose from the dead. And I can't believe that because I can't believe in miracles.

Chris: So let's talk about miracles. I respect your mind, Sal. You see how it all hangs together. Some people try to pick and choose what parts of Christianity they "feel comfortable with", as if Christians offered Christianity to the world as a comfort pill instead of as truth.

Sal: No Christianity without miracles, eh?

Chris: No such thing. Drop the miraculous element and you get a totally different religion.

Miracles essential to Christianity

Sal: Why?

Chris: Because everything distinctive to Christianity is a miracle. Creation, the Jewish prophecies of the Messiah, the Incarnation of God in Jesus, Jesus' own miracles, his Resurrection from the grave, and his return at the end of time: all the important events in the story are miracles. And Christianity is essentially a story, "good *news* ".

Sal: But other religions have miracle stories too, don't they?

Chris: Many others do, yes. But if you drop them out, the essential points remain intact in Islam and Confucianism and Taoism and Buddhism, and even Hinduism.

Sal: What about Judaism?

Chris: The Hebrew Scriptures are part of the Christian Scriptures, and they're full of miracles. It's the same God, after all, that Judaism and Christianity are about, the same God that the Old Testament and the New Testament are about.

Sal: This God is supposed to be perfect, right?

Chris: Right.

Sal: And he's supposed to have created the universe, right?

Chris: Right.

Sal: Well, why would a perfect God create a universe with so many imperfections in it that he has to perform miracles in it? That's like a plumber putting in a leaky pipe and then coming back to patch it up over and over again.

Miracles not afterthoughts   *Chris:* Oh, but miracles aren't leak-patches, not afterthoughts. They're masterstrokes of his art. They *fit*.

Sal: I don't see that. If the laws of nature are perfect, why does God make exceptions to them by miracles?

Chris: For the same reason any great artist makes exceptions to his general rules. Those rules aren't absolute. Do you really think the final, absolute rules of God's work are the little regularities our science has discovered so far?

Sal: Why not?

Chris: That's like thinking you understand a great painting because you've counted the little dots of color. A good artist is always wiser than you, and he surprises you. If you have him all figured out, then he's a little artist, not a great one. And God is a very great one.

Sal: So it's blind faith, this belief in miracles.

Chris: No indeed. After you get over the surprise, you understand it a little. After the miracles happen, you see their point. They're signs. The word for "miracle" in New Testament Greek means "sign". They point beyond themselves. They teach a lesson, reveal God. *Signs*

Sal: I like that. You don't need the miracle itself, then.

Chris: You do. If a sign weren't real, how could it teach you? First you look at it, then you look along it.

Sal: O.K., so miracles are to teach us something. What?

Chris: What God is like. Miracles of healing show us that God is a God of life and health, and wants us happy. They show us that God has both love and power, that those two things that are so often tragically separated in our lives are perfectly united in God. That's just one thing miracles teach us. There are more.

Sal: I have a problem with that—with God teaching us by miracles. They seem unworthy of what you mean by God.

Chris: Why?

Sal: They seem so crude, so primitive. Why should God need to put on a big show like that? It's . . . well, undignified.

Chris: If you saw one, would that help you believe?

Sal: Of course.

Chris: Then that's why God stoops from his dignity. He's a good teacher. He comes down to our level. He's no snob.

Sal: But people shouldn't need crude power displays to believe.

Chris: Perhaps not, but they do. *You* do, for one. You just said so yourself.

Sal: I? When?

Chris: When I asked, if you saw a miracle, would that help you believe? and you said yes.

Sal: Oh. You got me there. But even if miracles would be proper for God, they just don't happen.

Chris: That's what you *believe*, isn't it?

Sal: Yes.

Miracles and reason

Chris: Well, I think on this question of miracles you're the one who goes by faith and I'm the one who goes by reason and scientific evidence.

Sal: What? Why do you say that?

Chris: Because I have a lot of historical evidence on my side, and you have nothing but your unsupported conviction that "miracles just don't happen".

Sal: Wait a minute. I've got evidence too. I've heard of fake miracles, and I think you have too. If some were fake, why couldn't all be fake? We can be fooled, you know, just as we are by stage magicians.

Chris: That's like arguing that since you've seen some counterfeit money, why couldn't all money be counterfeit? A few fakes don't disprove the genuine article. If anything, they're a clue that there *is* a genuine article there to be imitated.

Sal: Well, I never saw any miracles.

Chris: And therefore you don't believe in them?

Sal: Right.

Chris: Then you'd better throw away your textbooks.

Sal: What do you mean?

Chris: Why do you believe your science or history or geography books? They tell you things you didn't see, like electrons and Caesar and Australia.

Sal: But people have seen those things. Reliable people. Many people.

Chris: And people have seen miracles. Reliable people. Many people.

Sal: No. The people who claim to see miracles are not reliable people, like scientists and historians.

Chris: Why aren't they reliable?

Sal: Why, because they claim to see miracles, of course!

Chris: Have you ever heard of "arguing in a circle"?

Sal: Oh. That *was* arguing in a circle, wasn't it?

Chris: Yes. It was just as silly as saying you don't believe in Australia even though many people say they've seen it, because those people must be unreliable, and then saying the reason they must be unreliable is because they say they've seen Australia.

Sal: But what solid historical evidence is there for miracles?

Chris: Plenty. Have you ever looked?

Sal: No.

Chris: Why not?

Sal: It would be a waste of time.

Chris: Because you know that miracles don't happen?

Sal: That's another circle, isn't it? Well, I *do* know miracles don't happen, because they'd violate the laws of nature. You can't believe in miracles and science at the same time.

Laws of nature

Chris: Yes you can. Let me try to explain. Would a presidential pardon to a criminal violate the laws of the court? Would a gift of extra money violate the laws of accounting? Would a hand adding food to a fish bowl violate the ecology of the fish bowl?

Sal: No, they just add to it.

Chris: Then why would miracles violate the laws of nature? They just *add* something. In fact, miracles *presuppose* the laws of nature. If there were no laws of nature, there couldn't be any distinction between natural events and miraculous events.

Sal: I see. But nature can't make miracles, can it?

Chris: No.

Sal: So it would have to be God who does miracles.

Chris: Right.

Sal: Well, then, how can human beings perform miracles? There are a lot of stories about them. Mustn't they all be false?

Chris: No human being can perform a miracle. But God can perform one through a human being as his instrument. A shovel can't dig a hole by itself, but I can use one to dig a hole.

Sal: I see. Well, here's what I think about those stories. They came from an age of ignorance of science and the laws of nature. What people in the past took to be miracles we can now explain scientifically. People came to believe in miracles only because they didn't know that clouds, not Zeus, made thunder and that tides, not Neptune, made tidal waves.

Chris: But miracle stories don't just come from the past. There are thousands of well-documented miracles today too.

Sal: Well, science will explain them too one day. What one age thinks of as miraculous, the next age explains by science.

Chris: You mean modern science says virgin births and resurrections from the grave and walking on water and through walls and feeding five thousand people from five loaves and two fishes aren't miraculous?

Sal: Some day science will explain them too, if they really happened.

Faith in science *Chris:* That's quite a faith you have. Science hasn't explained away a single real miracle in thousands of years, yet you believe that in the future it will explain away *all* miracles. You have as much faith in science as I have in God, it seems.

Sal: Science has explained some miracles.

Chris: Name one.

Sal: The parting of the Red Sea. A wind did that, not God.

Chris: Where did you get that idea?

Sal: Science, of course.

Chris: Wrong. You got it from the Bible.

Sal: What?

Chris: Exodus says it was a wind. But it also says it was God: "God raised up a wind".

Sal: Then that *wasn't* a miracle.

Chris: Perhaps not. But it was Providence: perfect timing.

Sal: Well, what about the virgin birth?

Chris: What about it?

Sal: Today we know all the details of the birth process. In an age of ignorance they could believe in a virgin birth. But no longer.

Chris: Really? You mean Mary and Joseph didn't know how babies are made? Come on now! What kind of chronological snob are you?

Chronological snobbery

Sal: What's a chronological snob?

Chris: Someone who looks down his nose not at other classes of people in the present but at all classes of people in the past. Someone who dismisses an idea not because it's proved to be untrue but just because more people in the past believed it than in the present. Someone who asks of an idea not whether it's *true* but whether it's *new*.

Sal: But they *didn't* know much science.

Chris: They didn't know all the details of how pregnancy worked inside a woman. But they certainly knew how it originated outside! A virgin birth is just as miraculous in 2,000 B.C. as in A.D. 2, and just as miraculous in A.D. 2 as in A.D. 2,000. You still haven't found a miracle that science has explained away.

Sal: What about faith healings? Modern psychology calls them psychosomatic. Our own mind can heal our body: the power of mind over matter.

Chris: Once again, that idea is taught in the Bible too. Jesus often says, "Your faith has healed you." Not all healings are miraculous. Many are psychosomatic. And the ancients knew at least as much about that as we do: about the power of mind over matter.

Sal: So *all* healings are psychosomatic then. You don't need God to explain them.

Chris: Not all. Raising the dead isn't psychosomatic. Or walking on water. Or feeding five thousand.

Sal: Well, I just don't believe they ever really happened.

Chris: That's an interesting statement about your private feelings, but it doesn't alter the facts, you know. The world doesn't wait for your beliefs to run the way it does.

Sal: Are you making fun of me?

Chris: No. Sorry if I seemed to. But I wanted you to see the point that you haven't given any *evidence*, any reasons for your belief. You go by tender, dreamy feelings—your feelings. I go by hard evidence. You go by your narrow-minded dogma. I have an open mind. Your philosophy doesn't allow you to believe in miracles. Mine does.

Sal: Hey! *I'm* supposed to be the hardheaded, open-minded scientist and *you're* supposed to be the prejudiced dogmatist.

Chris: I think you can see that that labeling itself is a prejudice. If you're open-minded enough to see it.

Sal: Hmmm. Most of the miracles you believe in are in the Bible, aren't they?

Chris: Yes. The ones I'm sure of, anyway.

Sal: Then we'd better talk about the Bible next. The main reason I never believed what the Bible said was because it was so full of miracles. Everything hangs together.

Chris: Yes, it does. See you tomorrow.

Dialogue Nine

The Bible:
Myth or History?

Sal: Chris, I've got to ask you something personal.

Chris: Go ahead, Sal. We're friends, aren't we?

Sal: How do you know so much about God? Are you a theological brain?

Chris: No, not at all. I'm just an ordinary person.

Sal: You must have taken some high level religion courses somewhere.

Chris: No . . .

Sal: Then you must have read hundreds of books.

Chris: No, Sal. Actually, what I know about God for sure comes from just one book. In fact, what the whole human race knows about God for sure, and not just as a matter of speculation and guesswork, comes from just one book.

Sal: The Bible, you mean?

Chris: Yes.

Sal: You really believe that one book gives you all the facts about God?

Chris: *All* the facts? Of course not. How could we ever have all the facts about the Infinite One? None of us can have complete knowledge of God, any more than a clam could have complete knowledge of us. Less so, in fact, because the difference between us and clams is only finite, but the difference between us and God is infinite.

Sal: *Some* facts, then?

Chris: Yes, what he told us.

Sal: So you think you've got some hard facts there in the Bible, eh?

Chris: I don't know what you mean by "hard facts".

Sal: Like the stuff science gives us.

Chris: No. Science measures things. We can't measure God.

Sal: So it's just myth, then.

Chris: No, it's truth.

Sal: You mean you really think God sits up there in the sky on a golden throne and has a strong right hand, and gets angry?

Chris: No. That's poetic language. But you can tell the truth in poetic language, you know. God really is exalted—though not physically, in space, in the sky. God really does rule the universe, though not from a physical golden throne. God really does have all power, though he doesn't have the same kind of strength as Muhammad Ali had in his right hand. And God really does want us to do good and not evil, though he doesn't get hysterical and red in the face.

Sal: So it's just symbolism.

Chris: But *true* symbolism. Not just a made-up story, like Santa Claus.

Sal: So you admit the whole Bible is poetic symbolism, not literal history.

Symbolic language   *Chris:* No, I didn't say that. I said that the language it uses to describe *God* has to be symbolic. God can't be described literally because we can't see him. He doesn't have a physical body. But there are a lot of things in the Bible that *are* described literally—things we *can* see.

Sal: How can you tell what parts of the Bible to interpret symbolically and what parts to interpret literally? Isn't it just your personal preference?

Chris: No, there's an objective standard.

Sal: Well, what is it?

Standard of interpretation

Chris: It's quite simple, really. Language about visible things is meant literally, language about invisible things is meant symbolically.

Sal: So the story of the creation of the world in Genesis is meant literally? It is about visible things, the universe.

Chris: But before the creation of Adam and Eve there was no human eye around to see it. So the account isn't an eyewitness account. It's true, but not literal. The "6 days" of creation, for instance, don't have to be 24 hour days.

Sal: And the last book in the Bible, the book of Revelation—all that stuff about the end of the world, horses and burning mountains going through the sky and angels blowing trumpets—that's not literal either, right?

Chris: Right. That's symbolism. But it's true. It'll happen, just as the creation happened.

Sal: But it's not literal because nobody's there to see it yet. It's future.

Chris: Well, prophecies of the future can be literal. You could predict something literally. Some passages in the Bible do. For instance, the Old Testament predicts dozens of specific details about the Messiah that happened, literally, to Jesus, like being sold for 30 pieces of silver, and having his clothes gambled for.

Sal: I guess I'm really concerned with whether you interpret the miracle stories literally or not.

Chris: If they're meant literally, yes.

Sal: Like Noah's flood and the ten plagues in Egypt and the crossing of the Red Sea? And all Jesus' miracles? And the literal Resurrection?

Chris: Yes.

Sal: Well, I don't.

Chris: Don't what?

Sal: Believe the miracle stories. So I don't interpret them literally, I interpret them symbolically.

Chris: You're confused, Sal.

Sal: You mean you think I'm wrong. But I'm not confused. I know what I believe and what I don't believe.

Interpretation and belief

Chris: No, I mean you're confused. You're confusing two different questions: interpretation and belief.

Sal: What do you mean?

Chris: The question of interpretation is: What did the writer mean? The question of belief is: Do you agree with him? The question of interpretation is: What does the Bible *claim* to be true? The question of belief is: What do you believe really is true?

Sal: Well, I interpret the Bible according to my beliefs.

Chris: But that's your confusion, Sal. Suppose I read a speech by Hitler that said we should create a super-race of Germans and kill all the Jews. Suppose I didn't believe that, so I interpreted the speech according to my beliefs and I said that what the speech really meant was that all races were equal and we should love one another. Do you see how I would be confused?

Sal: Not about race, or love.

Chris: But about what Hitler meant.

Sal: Oh. Yes. I see. But wouldn't it be good to improve on such a terrible speech?

Chris: If you want to make a speech yourself, yes. If you want to choose what to believe in, yes. But if you want to know what Hitler *meant*, no. That's your confusion. You think the Bible's stories of miracles are *false*. Why not just say so, clearly? The miracle stories are either lies or true history. They're not myth.

They're not *meant* mythically, or poetically, or symbolically.

Sal: But I think they are. What could be more poetic and symbolic than life coming out of death—Jesus' Resurrection is just like spring. And Moses' crossing the Red Sea is a perfect symbol for overcoming death, or any obstacle. There are all sorts of poetic, symbolic meanings in the miracles.

Chris: I agree. But that doesn't mean they aren't literal too. They're signs. But if a sign isn't really there—if there's no literal piece of wood on a pole—then it can't symbolize anything, can it? So if Moses didn't really cross the Red Sea, it's not a real sign of anything. I believe the miracles are signs and symbols, all right. But I also believe they really happened. They're not just stories, myths. You think that's all they are, right?

Sal: Right.

Chris: So you agree with the demythologizers. *Demythologizers*

Sal: What's that?

Chris: The word was made popular by a German theologian named Rudolf Bultmann. It means that the miracle stories are only myths, and that we should believe the rest of the Bible, but not the myths. A lot of theologians believe that. Many rabbis and priests and ministers do too. Some writers of catechism textbooks too.

Sal: So I'm in good company.

Chris: No, in *numerous* company. Truth isn't found by counting noses. I'd rather agree with God even if only a few human beings agreed with me, than agree with millions of humans but disagree with God.

Sal: Well, doesn't the clergy teach demythologizing? You said a lot of rabbis and ministers and priests believe it. Are they heretics?

Chris: Technically, yes. If they disagree with essential teachings of the Bible. But the word *heretic* isn't used much any more.

Sal: You sound sad. Do you want to burn heretics, like the Inquisition?

Chris: Of course not. You can label an idea accurately without wanting to burn the people who hold it.

Sal: I'm glad to hear that. Because I guess I'm a heretic. I think for myself. I don't just swallow whatever line the Church gives me.

Chris: Then you have your reasons for disagreeing?

Sal: Certainly.

Chris: I think you can guess what my next question is going to be.

Sal: We went over those reasons in that conversation we had about miracles.

Chris: Yes. You see, everything is connected. If there's no supernatural God with the power to work miracles, then miracles can't happen. If miracles can't happen, then Christ didn't really rise from the dead. If Christ didn't really rise from the dead, the story is only a myth, and the demythologizers are right. (Though they're still confusing the two questions of interpretation and belief; they should say the story is a *lie*, not a *myth*.) Do you have any other reasons, any new reasons for being a demythologizer of the Bible?

Sal: Yes, I do. I've been reading some books about this, and I think I've found at least four good reasons for being skeptical about the Bible.

Chris: Go ahead. What are they?

Form criticism   *Sal:* For one thing, there's what they call "form criticism". That means you should interpret a text not absolutely but relative to its literary form. If the form is poetry or myth or parable, you just don't take the story literally.

Chris: That's a good principle. So apply it to eyewitness descriptions too, and historical narratives, and interpret them literally, just as you interpret symbolism symbolically. The miracle stories have the form of history, not myth.

Sal: No they don't. And that's my second point: the resemblances between the Bible's miracle stories and myth. They're both full of magic. And things like magic numbers: ten plagues, forty days of fasting, three days in the tomb.

Magic

Chris: Do you mean to say no one ever really fasts forty days, and plagues can really come in any number but ten? Or that if Jesus had spent four days in the tomb you'd be more likely to believe it?

Sal: Well, no. But mustn't we distinguish two different questions, the question of belief and the question of history? That's my third point. Whether Moses really crossed the Red Sea or not is not important; that's the question of history. The important thing is whether or not God was there; the point of the Bible is religion, not history.

Chris: But the Bible's religion depends on history. Its God works in history. Your distinction between history and religion fits Oriental religions, but not Western religions. It's not important whether Buddha ever really lived; the only important thing is meditation and practicing Buddha's way. But Christianity is different: it's about Christ. If he never lived, or never died and rose again, then Christianity is simply a lie. Aren't you honest enough to call it that, if that's what you believe?

Sal: But it has so much good stuff to say about ethics and love and neighborliness.

Chris: Everybody knows that already, even though they don't practice it. Remember our first conversation? If ethics is all that Christianity means, forget it.

Sal: Why?

Chris: Because then it's just copying all the other good philosophies and moralities. It claims to be different; it claims to be history, "good news", Gospel: that God came to earth and died on the cross and rose again to save us from sin and death and Hell.

Sal: That's what *you* say it is.

Chris: That's simply what Christianity *is*, and always was from the beginning. If you don't believe that, you're not a Christian. Just agreeing with Jesus' ethics doesn't make you a Christian, any more than agreeing with Buddha's ethics makes you a Buddhist.

Sal: Well, I guess I'll have to say I'm not a Christian, then.

Chris: Good! That's the first step to becoming one.

Sal: But I still have another reason for not believing in the stories in the Bible. We haven't finished my four points, remember?

Chris: Sorry. What's the fourth one?

Contradictions in the Bible? *Sal:* There are contradictions in the Bible, internal inconsistencies in the stories. They can't all be true.

Chris: Name one.

Sal: Did Jesus speak the Sermon on the Mount all at once, as Matthew reports, or on different occasions, as Luke reports?

Chris: Why couldn't it be both? In any case Matthew didn't say Jesus said it *all at once*, he just said Jesus *said* it.

Sal: Well, what about the sign on the cross? How many words were on it? Each of the four Gospels has a different version.

Chris: Why couldn't they all be right, but some are condensed, sort of Reader's Digest versions, so to speak? If the sign really read, "This is Jesus of Nazareth, the King of the Jews", then the account that says simply "Jesus, King of the Jews" isn't *false*, just condensed. The essential point is the same. Show me a single contradiction about an essential point of substance, not just a matter of verbal style.

Sal: Well, they're *different*, anyway.

Chris: The very fact that the four Gospels tell the same story in different ways is strong evidence that the story is true—like four witnesses in court telling the story in four different ways. If they agreed word for word, you'd think they had made it up and collaborated beforehand. The differences don't amount to contradictions. And the four Gospels agree remarkably—more so, much more so, than any other set of ancient documents about any other ancient event.

Sal: But an event so long ago—isn't it likely that the telling of it got garbled, like the party game where you sit in a circle and tell a message around?—by the time it gets to the tenth person it's a completely different message.

Chris: That's why the Church wrote it down in the Bible, and preserved this book with infinite care.

Sal: Well, even so, no matter how carefully the book is preserved, it's just a book. Written by human beings. Their ideas about God.

Chris: That's the essential question about the Bible: Is it our ideas about God or is it God's ideas about us? Is it God's Word to us or our words about God?

God's Word or our words

Sal: Yes, that's the essential question all right. It's like the question about God: Did he create us in his image or do we create him in our image?

Chris: Yes, and that's like the essential question about the Christian story too: Is it the story of our search for God or the story of God's search for us? Is it God coming down in Christ, the "one way" down, or is it us trying to get up to God, with Christ just one of the many human ways up, one of many manmade religions?

Sal: At least we've got the questions straight. And I see that all these questions are parts of one question: the question about the Bible being God's Word or ours, the question about God being Creator or created by us, the question about Christ being God's way down or our way up, and the question about the Christian religion being the one divine way or just one of many human ways. It all fits together.

Chris: Did I fail to answer any of your reasons for not believing the Bible?

Sal: Well, no, not really.

Chris: Then your reason for not believing it must be something else than what we've talked about. We've clarified the question, but not your real motive for answering it "no".

Sal: What do you think my real motive is? Are you going to psychoanalyze me?

Chris: No, but I have a good guess, and I can only ask you to honestly ask yourself whether this guess is accurate or not. You want to believe the demythologizers, right?

Sal: Right.

Chris: Why? Because you don't believe in miracles, right?

Sal: Right.

The personal challenge

Chris: And why don't you believe in miracles? Because if miracles happen, then Christ really did rise from the dead, and then he is not just a human ideal but he is really God—everyone's God, your God too, Sal. Then he has claims on your soul and on your life, right here and now. Then you have to face him and repent, turn around, beg forgiveness, let him be your Lord rather than you being your own lord. That's not an easy or comfortable thing to do, and I'm not trying to put you down for not doing it. I'm just trying to help you be honest with yourself and know yourself. Only you can answer the question: Is that really your motive for not believing? The reason I suspect it is, is because none of your arguments seem to stand up. The house of your beliefs doesn't stand on rational foundations. All your arguments can be answered. You just *choose* to believe there's no God, or no miracles, or no Resurrection, or no salvation.

Sal: Maybe so, Chris. We're friends, so we have to be honest with each other. I appreciate your speaking so frankly about this—acquaintances have to be polite, but friends can say hard things to each other. And I have to be as honest with you as you were with me: I just don't know.

Chris: That's a wonderful discovery, Sal: that you don't know. That's the beginning of wisdom.

Dialogue Ten

Death

Sal: O.K., Chris, I've really got a question for you today: the hardest question I've asked so far, I think. It's a question I remember asking when I was only about six years old. Maybe that's why it's such a hard question, if you know what I mean.

Chris: I know: if you can answer a six-year-old's questions, you can answer any questions. What is it?

Sal: God loves us, right?

Chris: Right. That's not the question, is it?

Sal: No, I'm leading up to it, using the "Socratic Method", just like you. Now, love always wants what's best for the loved one, right?

Chris: Right.

Sal: So if I love you, I'll try to save your life if it's threatened, right?

Chris: Right.

Sal: And God can save anybody from dying, because he's all-powerful and can perform miracles, right?

Chris: Right.

Sal: So why does God let people die?

Chris: That *is* a good question. Let me ask *you* one in answer. Do you think death is the worst thing that can happen to you?

Sal: Sure. You lose everything by death.

Is death the worst thing?

Chris: Not everything. Not your soul. You see, there are two kinds of death: death of the body and death of the soul. I think you have in mind only the death of the body. That's certainly a terrible thing, but the death of the soul is even worse, because the soul is *you*.

Sal: I'm not so sure about that.

Chris: Well, here's another reason. The body lasts only eighty years or so. The soul lasts eternally.

Sal: I'm not sure of that either.

Chris: We should discuss that some other time. I think there are good, strong arguments for the immortality of the soul, for life after death. But let's talk about death today, because I think that's really bothering you, right?

Sal: Right. How did you know?

Chris: Usually there's more on our minds than in our mouths.

Sal: What do you mean by that?

Chris: Usually we have motives in asking a question that we don't say.

Sal: Well, you're right. I was shaken when I heard the news: Maggie died yesterday.

Chris: Maggie? Your friend? That's terrible, Sal. I'm so sorry.

Sal: Why did she have to die? She was so young!

Chris: Why do *any* of us have to die?

Sal: Why are you making my question harder?

Chris: I'm not. I don't know God's reasons for letting *her* die so young, but I know his reasons for letting us all die.

Sal: Who do you think you are, anyway? Have you got mental telepathy with God? How do you know God's reasons?

Chris: Same way you can know. He's told us.

Sal: I suppose you think you have a private telephone line to God?

Chris: Not at all. It's perfectly public. It's revealed.

Sal: In the Bible, you mean?

Chris: Yes. That old book we were talking about yesterday.

Sal: Everything connected again, I see. Well, why, according to the Bible, did Maggie have to die?

Chris: I told you, I don't know why she of all people, she in particular. But it tells us why we *all* have to die. Because we're sinners.

Sin: the reason for death

Sal: That's an awful answer! You mean God got so mad at us when we sinned that he killed us?

Chris: No.

Sal: But God does get mad at sinners. He hates sinners, right?

Chris: Wrong. He hates sin. He loves sinners. In fact, that's exactly the reason why he lets us die: because he loves us.

Sal: That makes no sense at all. When we love a person we certainly don't want to let them die. Not even an animal. How could love let us die?

Chris: Because physical death isn't the worst thing, and it's the only alternative to the one thing that's even worse: spiritual death. God allows the second worst thing to keep us from the first worst thing.

Sal: Explain. I don't get that.

Chris: Suppose we never died. Suppose we lived here forever, here on earth, in our present condition, as sinners, with the sickness of sin in our souls. You know what happens to a sickness, don't you? It spreads. So God put a tourniquet around it: after seventy or eighty years, more or less, we die. Sin can't cross the barrier of death with us. We can't sin anymore after death. Death is like a quarantine against sin.

Sal: That sounds like a pretty gloomy picture of us. Are we really such diseased creatures?

Chris: That's half the truth, yes. The other half is that we're made in God's image. We're very good *and* very bad. We're God's children but we're sinners.

Sal: I thought God loved us even if we're sinners.

Chris: Oh, he does. But we often don't accept that love and respond to it. It's like the sun shining all the time, but the shades are down, so we don't receive it. We have to get rid of the shades.

Sal: The shades symbolize sin?

Chris: Yes.

Sal: But nobody's perfect.

Chris: Exactly. And God designed us to be perfect. So we need a healing, an operation, to restore us to that design.

Sal: Perfection is unrealistic. Who could expect us to be perfect?

Chris: As we are now, it's unrealistic. But not as God originally designed us to be, and what he still destines us to be.

We will be perfect.   *Sal:* You mean we're still going to be perfect?

Chris: Yes.

Sal: Oh, come on!

Chris: That's not my idea. It's his.

Sal: Is that in the Bible?

Chris: It sure is. In the Old Testament, God commanded, "Be ye holy as I the Lord your God am holy." In the New Testament, Jesus commanded, "Be ye perfect, even as your Father in Heaven is perfect."

Sal: That's ridiculous. We can't do that.

Chris: No, we can't. That's what sin did to us. We can't become what God made us to be. We're all failures.

Sal: I don't feel like a failure.

Chris: That's because your feelings are failures too.

Sal: I don't feel my feelings are failures either.

Chris: Well, I go by God's Word, not by my feelings. My feelings aren't infallible.

Sal: Neither are mine. But I'm not a perfectionist.

Chris: But God is.

Sal: I'm satisfied with myself the way I am.

Chris: But God isn't.

Sal: I love myself the way I am. Doesn't God?

Chris: Yes, but he loves you much more than that too, much more than you love yourself.

Sal: How do you figure that? Perfectionism doesn't sound like love.

Chris: When an artist really loves one statue, or painting, or piece of music, isn't the artist much more of a perfectionist about it than about some old scraps, some practice junk?

Sal: Yes.

Chris: Well, you're not God's junk. You're God's art.

Sal: That's quite a compliment. But I still don't see why we have to die.

Chris: Because God wants to heal us. We need an operation to take away all the sin from our souls, and death is like the anesthetic for God's operation. Only after our death makes our will passive do we stop hopping around on God's operating table. We stop saying, "*My* will be done" instead of "Thy will be done" only at death. Death lets God into our inner being, our heart. We become totally defenseless and open and vulnerable then.

Sal: So death is good, then?

Chris: It's not good that it has to exist, but given the disease of sin, it's good. It's good as an operation is good. It would be better if it weren't needed. But since it is needed, it's better that it exists than not.

Sal: But why do we need this operation? Did God create junk after all? Did he design us with a dark side, a sin side, a death side?

The origin of sin   *Chris:* No. He made us perfect. *We* brought sin and death into the world.

Sal: You mean you really believe that Garden of Eden story?

Chris: Yes, I do.

Sal: I thought that was only poetic symbolism.

Chris: Even if it is, it's true. Maybe the talking snake and the forbidden fruit are symbols, but they symbolize something that really happened.

Sal: What really happened?

Chris: First, God made us perfectly good, then we really chose evil instead. If you deny either of those two happenings, you make God the one to blame for evil instead of us.

Sal: What was the forbidden fruit? Sex?

Chris: What a silly idea! Why would you think that? God made sex, just as he made everything else that's good, and he told us how to use it, in marriage. His first command was, "Be fruitful and multiply."

Sal: What does the forbidden fruit symbolize then?

Chris: Remember in the story there are two special trees in the garden: the Tree of Life—that's eternal life, Heavenly life—and the Tree of the Knowledge of Good and Evil. ("Knowledge" means "experience" here, not just mental knowledge.) Adam and Eve chose the fruit of the wrong tree, the forbidden tree. So now they experience evil as well as good. So God exiled them from the garden "lest they eat of the Tree of Life and live forever". They were denied eternal life because of sin.

Sal: Sounds like a pretty stiff penalty for one apple.

Chris: It doesn't say it was an apple.

Sal: Whatever. You mean we have to die just because Eve ate a fruit?

Chris: Now you're interpreting the story only literally. Whether the first sin was literally eating a fruit or not, is not the most important point. The point is that we lost eternal life by sinning against God.

Sal: Just for that one little act?

What sin is

Chris: No. Sin is not just an act but also a state of being. That act brought about the state of separation from God, just as the act of running away or divorce can bring about the state of separation in a family. "Sin" means "separation from God".

Sal: So now we're a different kind of person than before?

Chris: Yes. Now we're sinners. And that's why we sin. We sin because we're sinners, just as we sing because we're singers.

Sal: So God gave us death to punish us?

Chris: To heal us. We need death to get rid of sin.

Death removes sin.

Sal: Is that all we need to do to get rid of sin? Just die?

Chris: No. We have to repent and believe before we die. But if we do, then death completes God's healing operation on our sin, on our separation.

Sal: Death reunites us to God?

Chris: Yes. Death is like the golden chariot sent by the king to fetch his Cinderella bride to his castle, where she lives with him happily ever after.

Sal: That's beautiful, but I wonder whether we really need death. Why couldn't God just let us live forever?

Chris: We went over that before: that would mean living forever separated from God.

Sal: I guess I don't quite understand that. I thought God knew us and loved us and took care of us now. How are we separated from God now?

Chris: We're separated from the experience of his love and joy and goodness. That's why we look around so desperately for substitutes to make us happy. That's why we sin: we idolize things, or power, or pleasure, or reputation; they're substitutes for God. If we had God, if we lived in love and communion with him every moment, we'd never sin. We couldn't be tempted by bad substitutes if the Real Thing were really present.

Sal: You mean sin is loving something else as if it were God?

Chris: Yes. We can't live without love and without joy. If we don't have God's love and joy, we have to look for it somewhere else. So we treat something in the world or something in ourselves as God, as the most important thing in our life, as the thing we love most, the thing we hope in as our joy and happiness. And it never works.

Sal: Sure it does. Different strokes for different folks, they say. You religious people get your kicks out of God, other people get theirs out of something else. It's a free country.

Chris: It just won't work.

Sal: What won't?

Chris: Looking for joy in anything else besides God.

Sal: Why not?

Happiness without God?

Chris: Because you can't fill an infinite hole with a finite thing. You can no more fill the hole in your heart with something in yourself or your world than you can fill the Grand Canyon with a few marbles.

Sal: I can try.

Chris: Yes, you can. And experience is an honest teacher, if you honestly listen to it. It will show you what I just said. You don't have to take it on my authority. Ask your own heart: Are you ever completely satisfied, deep down totally happy?

Sal: I don't think anybody is.

Chris: Then you should be in the market for God.

Sal: I don't know. The way you make it sound, God's like a crutch.

Chris: Sure he is! And we're spiritual cripples.

Sal: That's what I can't admit.

Chris: Oh, but you just did. You admitted you couldn't make your own heart perfectly happy. That's the bad news. The good news is that God can, and wants to, and will, if only we let him.

Sal: How can he do that?

Chris: Let him do it and you will know.

Immortality

Sal: Chris?

Chris: Yes, Sal.

Sal: Is there really a Heaven?

Chris: You really want to know, don't you?

Sal: Yes. How did you know that?

Chris: You came right out and asked that question simply and directly, like a child.

Sal: Is that bad?

Chris: No, that's good.

Sal: And have you got a good answer?

Chris: Yes.

Sal: What's the answer?

Chris: I just told you. The answer is yes.

Sal: How do you know?

Chris: Jesus told me.

Sal: How am *I* supposed to know?

Chris: Same way. He told everybody. It's no secret.

Sal: Well, it is to me. I'm still looking.

Chris: Then you'll find it. He promised that: "All who seek, find."

Sal: I guess everybody finds out when they die. But I want to know now.

Chris: That's certainly reasonable. Why wait until it's too late?

Sal: It's not just for my own sake that I want to know.

Chris: You're concerned about Maggie, aren't you?

Sal: Yes. I want to know that she still *is*, still really *is* somewhere. I feel that very strongly, but I want to know it.

Chris: Well, you're right. She is.

Sal: I know she still lives in our memories.

Do the dead still live? *Chris:* No, more than that—she really is. Alive. There's life after death.

Sal: How can you be so sure?

Chris: I told you: Jesus. But if you want other reasons, I'll give you some, but please remember they aren't my main reasons. My faith in life after death isn't based on arguments.

Sal: But your faith can express itself in arguments.

Chris: Yes.

Sal: So what are they?

Chris: Well, a first one is based on authority.

Sal: I'm suspicious of authority.

Chris: Like parents, and textbooks, and scientists, and newspapers?

Sal: Yes. I'm suspicious of them. They're not infallible.

Chris: True. But most of the things we learn, we learn from reliable authorities.

Sal: O.K., so it's reasonable to trust reliable authorities. So how does that prove life after death?

What authorities say *Chris:* Most of the authorities teach it: most of the philosophers and sages and saints. And common people too. Christians are with the wise and with the majority here.

Sal: The majority of the past. Not any more. Most people are skeptical today.

Chris: Not *most* people, just more people. But even if *all* the people today were skeptical, believers still make up the vast majority of all people.

Sal: How?

Chris: Most people are dead, you know. Let them have a vote too.

Sal: They didn't know science.

Chris: So what? How does science disprove life after death?

Sal: It seems to.

Chris: Which science? Which discovery? What facts that the ancients didn't know and you do disprove life after death?

Sal: Well . . . I can't tell you any one in particular. It's just the scientific climate of opinion.

Chris: You can rely on "climates of opinion" if you want. I'll rely on clear and definite facts and reasons. Which attitude do you think is more scientific?

Sal: What facts? Have you ever died? Have you ever been to Heaven and back? If not, how can you claim to know about it?

Chris: Because I have a good friend who has, and I believe him.

Sal: Jesus, you mean?

Chris: Yes.

Sal: Him again. It always comes back to him.

Chris: Yes, it does.

Sal: Well, what are your other arguments for believing in life after death?

Chris: I don't need any more, but if you do, here's a second one, a clue from nature. Ever hear of the conservation of energy?

A clue from nature

Sal: Sure. It means that no energy is ever totally destroyed, just changed. How does that make for a clue?

Chris: If even physical energy isn't destroyed, why should spirits be destroyed?

Sal: You mean the immortality of the soul is sort of the spiritual equivalent to the conservation of energy?

Chris: Yes. It's more a clue than an argument. Like a sign. It points to something. And evolution is another sign in nature that seems to point to life after death.

Sal: How?

Chris: If nature took millions, perhaps billions of years to evolve us, as her most advanced and most conscious life form, then for us to die forever would be like a sculptor taking years to sculpt his masterpiece and then destroying it. If we're nurtured in the womb of Mother Nature only to die, we're the cosmic abortion.

Sal: That would be awful. But it doesn't *prove* life after death, you know.

Chris: No, but it's a clue. It shows that either there's life after death or the universe is absurd.

Sal: Have you got any more arguments, or clues?

Dying as a birth   *Chris:* Here's a third one. Birth seems like death, and death therefore like birth. The process of being born is very much like the process of dying. Maybe the unborn child wonders whether there's life after birth. Death seems to be like a mother, then, birthing us into a larger world.

Sal: You mean this whole universe is only a womb in a bigger world?

Chris: Yes. Look! All of life is full of the clues that death is like birth. Life progresses by dying: you die to your mother's womb, to nursing at her breast, to the nursery, the kindergarten, each grade in school, home, family, old jobs, old cities, to move on to new ones. We're like three-stage rockets. Each stage dies and sets the next one flying: from the womb to this world and from this world to the next.

Sal: A beautiful idea, but again only a clue, not a proof.

The soul   *Chris:* Yes, but here's a fourth one, an argument from the nature of the human soul.

Sal: What do you mean by the human soul?

Chris: Your *you*, your personality, your thoughts and feelings. Everything in you that has no size, shape, weight, or color. The nonmaterial aspect of you. Not *what* you are but *who* you are.

Sal: Suppose I don't admit I have a soul? Maybe I'm just a *what*, not a *who*.

Chris: Then who's admitting that? Who's thinking there's no thinker?

Sal: Oh.

Chris: And if you have no soul, what goes out of your body when you die?

Sal: Life.

Chris: Is that something material? Does it have weight?

Sal: No. A dead body weighs the same as a living body.

Chris: Then that's one of the things the soul is: life.

Sal: O.K., so I have a soul. That doesn't mean it's immortal.

Chris: But think of what it is. It's so different from the body that bullets or cancer can't kill it.

Sal: They kill my body all right.

Chris: Yes. But why should the destruction of one thing be the destruction of a different kind of thing?

Sal: What do you mean?

Chris: When you mix oil and water, you can burn away the oil and the water won't burn. Or you can evaporate away the water but not the oil. The death of one thing doesn't mean the death of another. So the death of the body doesn't mean the death of the soul.

Sal: But oil and water can both be destroyed, although in different ways. How do you know the soul can't be destroyed in a different way?

Chris: As a matter of fact, it can.

The soul can die.

Sal: Souls can die?

Chris: Yes, in Hell.

Sal: I was afraid of that.

Chris: Good. If there's anything in all of reality to be afraid of, that's it.

Sal: I didn't mean I was afraid of Hell. I meant I was afraid you'd bring it up. I don't believe in Hell.

Chris: Let's save that topic for another conversation, O.K.?

Sal: O.K.

Chris: Here's another version of the argument from the nature of the soul and how different it is from the body. Do you think you cut pieces off your soul when you cut your nails, or get a haircut?

Sal: Of course not. That's silly.

Chris: Why?

Sal: Because the soul isn't the sort of thing you can cut up.

Chris: Exactly. It's not measurable in inches. It has no spatial parts.

Sal: So?

Chris: So it can't fall apart, which is how the body dies. The body's atoms and molecules and tissues and organs stop working together and start to fall apart. Eventually the corpse decays into millions of particles, all separate from each other. But the soul can't fall apart because it has no parts. It's not made of atoms.

Sal: What's it made of?

Chris: Consciousness. Thought, will, feeling. A different sort of thing.

Sal: That makes sense. Is that your strongest argument?

Chris: No. Here's a fifth one. I'm putting them in order from weaker to stronger. This one is from the nature of God. It tells us the real reason why the soul is immortal: because God made it immortal. He did this for three reasons: because he's just, loving, and creative.

Sal: Wait a minute. If someone doesn't believe in God, this argument isn't going to convince them.

Chris: Of course not. But it tells us the real reason why we're immortal. First, because God is just; and final, complete justice isn't done in this life.

Sal: That's for sure. The evil aren't punished and the good aren't rewarded.

Chris: That's why there has to be a next life: for justice. A second reason is God's creativity. He just likes life. He made a lot of it. He prefers life to death. That's why we do too: we're made in his image. Finally, a third reason, the most important one, is his love. If you love someone, you don't want him to die.

God loves life.

Sal: But we *do* die!

Chris: Our bodies die.

Sal: Chris, these five arguments sound good, but they just seem too abstract for me. I wish you could argue from something in my experience.

Chris: I just did. Love.

Sal: That's *God's* love. I experience only human love.

Chris: That gives you an argument too, a sixth one. When you really love someone, you see that he is irreplaceable, indispensable. If he dies forever, then life is an outrageous horror. It treats people like diapers. It dispenses with the indispensable. It replaces the irreplaceable.

Human love a clue to immortality

Sal: That's awful, but that's not a proof of immortality.

Chris: Almost. It proves that either we're immortal or life is outrageous. Six million Jews die in Hitler's gas ovens—is that all there is? Is life just as Macbeth says?

Sal: What did Macbeth say?

Chris: "Tomorrow, and tomorrow, and tomorrow,
Creeps in this petty pace from day to day
To the last syllable of recorded time;
And all our yesterdays have lighted fools
The way to dusty death. Out, out, brief
candle!
Life's but a walking shadow, a poor player
That struts and frets his hour upon the stage
And then is heard no more. It is a tale
Told by an idiot, full of sound and fury,
Signifying nothing."

Sal: It's either Macbeth's despair or life after death, is it?

Chris: Yes.

Sal: And that's your strongest argument?

Chris: No. My strongest argument will take another whole conversation, I think. But remember, none of these arguments is my main reason for believing.

Sal: That's Jesus, right?

Chris: Right. Jesus' Resurrection from the dead takes life after death out of the realm of philosophy and argument and speculation and puts it into the realm of visible fact. It really happened. We saw it.

Sal: "We"?

Chris: The Church. The Church is the witness to Christ's Resurrection. She preaches the "good news" she saw almost 2,000 years ago. I'm not so much arguing with you as announcing the news and inviting you to believe it.

Sal: It *is* inviting. But I want to hear your seventh argument first.

Chris: Tomorrow.

Dialogue Twelve

Longing

Chris: Sal, let's start today's conversation with a question. Suppose you were God and you could do anything at all. You could give yourself anything you want. You could design a Heaven for yourself. What would it be like?

Sal: Wow! That's some question. Why do you ask me that?

Chris: Never mind; that'll come clear later. But what do you really want most? What do you long for more than anything else you can imagine? If you could have anything you desire, what would it be?

Sal: I really don't know.

Chris: I thought so.

Sal: You mean you thought I was stupid?

Chris: No, I mean I thought you were honest. I think everybody's in that situation. We all want something but we don't know what it is.

What people really want

Sal: *Some* people seem pretty content with what they already have.

Chris: Deep down? I wonder. For one thing, they want more of what they have. Life, for one thing. They don't want to die. Time—they want more time. There's never enough time—enough time fully to love and know and appreciate and explore anything—any person or place or thing.

113

Sal: I know what you mean. I wish I could have spent years at that great vacation place I went to last year. And not *places* most of all, but *people*. When you're in love, you just never get enough of the other person; you want to be with that person forever, and keep getting closer and closer, and it never seems to end.

Chris: You know exactly what I mean, then. And sometimes there's something else—not a person or a place or a thing, but something that seems to show *through* them, something they point to, a sort of hint or whisper, or rumor—almost like a smell, a feel— do you know what I mean? What you long for isn't the place itself. Because if you get there, you still long for something else. Even if the place isn't disappointing, even if it's the greatest spot in the world, it just doesn't satisfy that other longing, the one that comes *through* it.

Sal: I wonder if all people feel it. They don't seem to.

Chris: I think they do. They can't talk about it unless they're really good friends who understand each other deeply. So they keep it covered up. Because it's embarrassing. It makes them feel vulnerable and defenseless and soft, like a child.

Sal: I feel that way when I listen to certain pieces of music. Sometimes I even feel scared I'll come apart and not get back together again—like I don't know who I am, almost like my soul forgot to stay in my body. Is that making any sense at all?

Chris: More than you can imagine.

Sal: Do you think anybody else understands that?

The world's best-kept secret   *Chris:* Yes, in different ways. I think *everybody* I ever met is keeping the world's best hidden secret: that *nobody* in this whole world is really, really happy, totally content. Everybody's looking for something, everybody's longing for something. A piece of everybody's heart is restless.

Sal: Oh, now I know why you brought this up. I remember that famous quotation from Saint Augustine, where he says to God, "You have made us for yourself, and that's why our hearts are restless until they rest in you." You think this restlessness proves the existence of God?

Chris: No, not *proves* God; *leads* to God sometimes. But I wanted to use it as the basis of my last argument for Heaven, for life after death, for immortality.

Sal: I don't see how this proves Heaven.

Chris: But you admit that nothing on earth totally satisfies you? That everything you've ever felt has felt like only a hint, or glimpse, or shadow of what you most deeply long for?

Sal: It feels like that. But that doesn't prove anything. It doesn't prove Heaven exists. Maybe it's just wishful thinking. We desire hundreds of things we never get, like a million dollars. Some of them we can't ever get, like 1,000 years of life.

Chris: Yes, but do we desire things that don't exist?

Sal: How could we? That would be meaningless.

Chris: Exactly. If they don't exist, we can't know them, and if we can't know them, we can't desire them. But we do desire this something more than earth can ever give us. Therefore it must exist.

Sal: Wait a minute. How do you know this something is Heaven? I don't want golden streets and harps and jewelry.

Chris: Neither do I. Those are only symbols of it. We'll talk about what Heaven is really like next time, if you want. My point now is that this desire is natural, innate, implanted in all of us. And every natural desire has a real object somewhere. So this one must too. And that object is nowhere on earth. So it must be in Heaven.

Every natural desire has a real object.

Sal: Wait a minute. I'm not sure every desire has a real object.

Chris: Every natural, innate desire does. Every desire that comes from our own nature has an object. Other desires come from outside: from advertising, or friends, or made-up fantasies, like Superman. If you want to fly like Superman, that doesn't mean you or anybody else ever will. But every natural desire is like an arrow pointing to a real object. We get hungry because there's real food. We get thirsty because there's real drink. We have sexual desires because there's really another sex. We get lonely because there really is friendship and society. We get curious because there really is truth.

Sal: O.K., I admit that every natural desire has a real object.

Chris: And this mysterious desire we started talking about—the desire that no object on earth ever completely satisfies—is a natural desire, one that comes out of our very nature.

Sal: Yes.

Chris: Do you see what that proves?

Sal: Yes. If every natural desire proves its object and the desire for something more than earth is natural, then something more than earth must exist. But that doesn't prove we'll ever get there.

Chris: I didn't say it did. I wish it did. Getting hungry doesn't prove you won't starve either. But it proves that food exists.

Sal: O.K., but are you sure everyone has this desire? If it's natural, it's got to be in everybody, right?

Chris: Right.

Sal: Well, I'm not sure it's in everybody.

Something more than time *Chris:* Then why is everybody impatient with time? Why do we want more time, something more *than* time?

Sal: I can't believe we don't belong in time.

Chris: Suppose you found some birds who complained about the air, or some fish who complained about the sea. That would be like us. We complain about time. But we live surrounded by time. Everything in the world is in time. Our bodies and even our souls are in time. (It takes time to think and to feel, just as it takes time to breathe or to walk.) And we complain about time. Now what would you think about fish who complained about the ocean?

Sal: That they were foolish.

Chris: Or that they were about to become amphibians, destined to become amphibians. If they long for another environment, it must exist.

Sal: Unless . . . unless every other desire has a real object, but this one's the exception. Why couldn't that be? There are exceptions to every rule. So the rule about all the other desires doesn't prove that his desire isn't the exception.

Chris: No. But just think what that would mean. It would mean that the whole world is so carefully arranged that every human desire but one has an object, and that one is the greatest of all, the one we'd rather have satisfied than any other. It's the final one, the biggie, the conquest of death and time. If reality says "no" to this one and "yes" to every other one, then I'll tell you what reality is like. It's like a chef who gives you a great twelve-course dinner, and just after ten appetizers, when you're ready for the main course, he flushes it down the toilet.

Is the world a cruel trick?

Sal: That's terrible!

Chris: Exactly. That's what reality is like if there's no Heaven: a carefully arranged trick. We're lured on by thousands of appetizers—music and sunsets and human love and babies and spring—and then let down in the end. So if that's what it's like, then there's a God after all: a very bad God, a cosmic sadist, who baits his traps with poems and flowers and people and then snaps them shut forever at death.

Sal: Have you proved that that isn't so?

Chris: No, but have you proved that it is?

Sal: No . . .

Chris: Then you're free to choose to believe in the good God instead of the bad God. It's a good choice, a good gamble. You have nothing to lose and everything to win.

Sal: Why not *no* God?

The choice: good God or bad God

Chris: Who baits the traps then? It's too carefully arranged to be mere chance. Who sets up all the appetizers? No, it's either the good God or the bad God. I haven't *proved* it's the good God, but I've tried to bring you to the point of seeing what your choice is, what your options are. It's up to you to choose to believe.

Sal: I've got to think about this one for a long time. A lifetime maybe.

Chris: No, not that long. Part of your lifetime's over. And the rest of it isn't infinitely long. So at some time —a time you can't know—it's going to be too late.

Sal: I don't like to hear that kind of stuff.

Chris: Maybe not. But does that make it untrue?

Sal: No. It's true.

Chris: Remember what we agreed about truth?

Sal: Yes. I have to look at it, face it, if I'm going to be honest.

Chris: That's your first choice. Your second one, once you look, is whether to believe or not. I think a lot of people never make the second choice because they don't make the first one. They don't believe not because they've looked and found nothing, but because they didn't look.

Sal: Well, I'm looking. I don't know what I'm looking for, but I'm looking. And if it *is* God I'm looking for, if it is God I'm really longing for even though I don't know it, then I'm going to find him according to you, right? "Seek and you shall find"—that's his promise, isn't it?

Chris: Yes, Sal, that's his promise.

Heaven

Sal: Chris, you said in our last conversation that you think everyone longs for Heaven. I'm not sure of that. Isn't it only escapists who think about Heaven?

Chris: What do you mean by "escapists"?

Sal: People who can't make it down here. People who are unhappy with earth. They believe in Heaven because it gives them something to hope for as a compensation for a miserable life on earth.

Chris: I think you're right except for one word.

Sal: Really? What word?

Chris: "Only". I think there *are* some "escapists" who believe in Heaven for that reason. But it isn't *only* escapists who believe in Heaven and long for Heaven. Do I seem to be an escapist?

Sal: No.

Chris: No, I love this earth and this life and this body. And so do most Christians I know. Yet we believe in Heaven and long for it because it's even better than earth, much better. Just because one thing is good, that doesn't mean there can't be something even better. And just because some people may believe in a thing for bad reasons, that doesn't mean that thing doesn't really exist.

Christians are not escapists.

121

Sal: But don't you think that the stronger your belief in Heaven is, the more you ignore earth? *Mustn't* the idea of Heaven be escapist?

Chris: No. Why should it? A pregnant woman pays more attention to her unborn baby if she hopes it will see life after birth than if she thought it was going to be born dead, doesn't she?

Sal: Of course, but I don't see the connection.

Chris: This world is like a great big womb. At death we're born into a bigger and better world. If you don't believe in life after death, then life in this world is a miscarriage. And then it becomes *less* important, less valuable, not more—just like the pregnant woman's stillborn baby. Then life is cheap and meaningless in the long run even though it's valuable and meaningful in the short run, because in the long run it all goes down the drain.

Sal: That sounds right in theory, but it hasn't worked out that way in practice, has it? People who believed in Heaven have usually been escapists, throughout history.

Chris: No they haven't. Most of the people who loved this earth and this life the most, who contributed to human happiness on earth the most—most of those people have believed in Heaven.

Sal: Who?

Chris: Jesus, for one. And his followers.

Sal: Isn't it true that Christians failed to abolish slavery and other evils in this world because they were thinking only of the next world?

Chris: No, it isn't true. In fact it *was* Christians who abolished slavery. That's a good example of how Heaven is relevant to earth. It's always been the people who believed most strongly in Heaven who improved our lives on earth the most. Can you see why?

Sal: No. Why?

Chris: Because they were looking at earth as Heaven's colony. They tried to make the colony like the home-land. If you believe Heaven is your home, you don't neglect earth; you make it more like your home, just as an Englishman who loves England makes the jungle colony he lives in as English as he can.

Sal: That's clever, but I think that's just the way *you* think, not the way most Christians think.

Chris: What's the most familiar prayer to Christians?

Sal: The Lord's Prayer. The "Our Father".

Chris: Right. And we pray in that prayer—the prayer we pray all the time, the prayer Jesus taught us—"Thy kingdom come . . . on earth as in Heaven." Heaven is earth's model.

Sal: O.K. but how? What do you do in Heaven that's the model for earth? How can an eternal church service be relevant to life on earth?

"Relevance" of Heaven

Chris: Heaven isn't a church service. In fact, the book of Revelation says there's no church or temple building in Heaven at all, because God himself is there.

Sal: Well, what is it, then? What do you do in Heaven? And why isn't it boring? And how is it relevant to earth?

Chris: Three excellent questions, and I think the an-swer to all three of them is the same. We do the same essential things in Heaven that we're supposed to do on earth, only we do them perfectly.

What do we do in Heaven?

Sal: You mean like making money and driving cars and cooking food?

Chris: No. I said the same *essential* things. I think there are only three essential things we're all here to do: to know and love ourselves, each other, and God. Heaven is the perfecting and completing of those three things.

Sal: Can you be more specific?

Chris: It's not easy, because God didn't tell us much about what Heaven is like, so it's mostly speculation. But it can be disciplined speculation, imagination disciplined by what we *do* know from God's revelation and disciplined by reason . . .

Sal: Why didn't God tell us more about Heaven?

Chris: Because we can't understand it. If you could talk to an unborn baby, how much could you make it understand about life after birth? Not much. And this life is to the baby what Heaven is to us.

Sal: So you think there's more progress and growth and change after death?

Chris: I think so, yes. At the moment of death, we're still not perfect. Even though God knows and loves us perfectly, and accepts us without reservation if we're in Christ, still *we* haven't yet learned to know and love *him* perfectly yet, or our neighbors, or even ourselves. So my guess is that we learn those three lessons, go through those three growth processes, after death. We begin them here.

Sal: Do you think they happen together, all at once?

Chris: I don't know, but I think one at a time. I think we first have to learn everything about ourselves and our life on earth. You know, that's what seems to happen to people when they die. At the moment of dying, many people say they see their whole life pass before them with perfect clarity. I think that's God teaching them the meaning of everything that ever happened to them.

Purgatory   *Sal:* Don't Catholics believe most people have to go to Purgatory first before they can go to Heaven?

Chris: Maybe not *instead* of Heaven. Maybe Purgatory is like Heaven's bathroom, where you get washed before dinner. Maybe this vision of their lives that people see at death *is* Purgatory, where their soul is purged or purified and made holy and ready for Heaven. Like remedial reading of our earthly life.

Sal: So Purgatory wouldn't be a separate place from Heaven? That sounds Protestant rather than Catholic. Don't Catholics say you have to pay for your sins in Purgatory?

Chris: No. Christ did that on the cross. Purgatory is for rehabilitation, not retribution. Saint Catherine of Genoa said that the worst sufferings in Purgatory were more joyful than the greatest joys on earth because God is there teaching you and you want to learn everything he teaches you, even about your sins. It hurts, but it's the truth. You love the truth. That's why you're there in the first place.

Sal: I thought you got to Heaven by loving God, not truth.

Chris: God is truth.

Sal: You mean truth is God?

Chris: No, I mean God is truth. Truth is one of his attributes, as light is an attribute of the sun. If you love the sunlight, you really love the sun, even if you've never seen the sun directly.

God is truth.

Sal: You mean you can get to Heaven without Jesus? Just by loving truth in general?

Chris: No. Jesus clearly says he's the only way.

Sal: Then I don't understand what you just said.

Chris: Let's save that for another conversation. I think we should finish this one first, about what Heaven is like. O.K.?

Sal: O.K. Once you know yourself perfectly, through "Purgatory", what then?

Chris: Then you're mature enough to know and love others as you never could on earth. Then you can complete "The Communion of Saints".

The Communion of Saints

Sal: How's that done?

Chris: By means of communication we hardly dream of.

Sal: Mental telepathy?

Chris: Perhaps.

Sal: Do you think we'll have bodies?

Chris: I know we will.

Sal: How do you know that?

Chris: Jesus.

Sal: He taught it?

Chris: His Church and his disciples taught it, for instance Paul in 1 Corinthians 15. But Jesus did more than teach it; he *did* it. His body resurrected. So will ours.

Sal: I know we talked about this before, but it boggles my mind. How does God bring a dead body back to life?

Chris: It boggles my mind too. But then, how did God create this whole incredible, enormous universe out of nothing? If he can do the big miracle, he can certainly do the smaller one.

Spirit and body   *Sal:* Why would he *want* to bring dead bodies back to life? Why not just immortal souls?

Chris: For the same reason he gave us bodies in the first place. He just likes matter. A lot of it. He certainly created a lot of it. And he likes us as we are: humans, not angels. We didn't get put into bodies by mistake. We don't change our species after death.

Sal: Wouldn't it be better if we did?

Chris: God didn't think so. Why do you?

Sal: I thought spirit was better than matter. Aren't angels better than humans?

Chris: Not necessarily. They can be worse. A devil is a fallen angel. The work of Hell is purely spiritual, you know; it can't make a single atom of matter. Only God can. The Devil can only work in your spirit, your soul, by temptation and deception. Matter is good.

Sal: Well, then do you think people in Heaven are fully human?

Chris: Yes. More fully human than they ever succeeded in being here on earth.

Sal: Then they have emotions too?

Chris: I think so. All the good emotions, anyway, all the emotions that are part of being fully human.

Sal: I was going to ask whether they ever felt sorrow, but that's not a good emotion, is it?

Chris: It's good for us to feel sorrow now when other people suffer. But in Heaven "God will wipe away all tears from their eyes". There will be no reason to feel sorrow there.

Sal: But if you don't know sorrow, how can you appreciate joy?

Chris: We know plenty of sorrow here. Maybe that's one of the reasons we're here. Maybe that's why God doesn't just take us all to Heaven instantly. He wants to train us to appreciate it better first, to increase our joy in Heaven. Maybe for every ounce of sorrow on earth there's a million pounds more joy for each of the millions in Heaven.

Sal: Oh! Do you believe there are millions of people in Heaven right now?

Chris: Probably, yes. I don't have the population statistics.

Sal: Can they see us here?

Chris: Why not?

Sal: I can't see them.

Chris: That doesn't mean they can't see you.

Sal: You mean Moses might be watching me right now? You mean my dead grandmother might be watching me right now, knowing what we're saying and even thinking?

Chris: Yes.

Sal: How?

Chris: I don't know. Perhaps a little mental telepathy with God.

Sal: Isn't that just wishful thinking on your part?

A cloud of witnesses *Chris:* No. The Bible seems to teach it. It says in the book of Hebrews that "we are surrounded by a great cloud of witnesses", meaning the holy men and women of the past.

Sal: That makes me feel uncomfortable, and ashamed, if I'm being watched by so many eyes. There's no privacy then. Are you sure this is really true?

Chris: I'm sure *God* is watching us now, every minute, anyway. So your feeling is correct. There is no privacy. Whether God shares this knowledge of us with people in Heaven, I'm not so sure. But I know he knows each of us right down to the depths of our most secret heart and thoughts. And *that* certainly makes Heaven relevant to earth. You behave differently if you know you're being watched. And differently again if you know the watcher is Perfect Love.

What will we have? *Sal:* What do you think we'll have in Heaven? Music? Clothes? Pets? Books? Games?

Chris: Anything we want. Our wants will be completely good and wise then, not partly foolish and sinful and self-destructive, as they are now, so God will be able to give us everything we want. And if we want those things, we'll have them. Maybe we'll even have miraculous powers. He'll be able to trust us with them then.

Sal: It seems strange to think of animals in Heaven.

Chris: Why? Would you rather have none?

Sal: No.

Chris: Well, then, whatever Heaven is like, it will be better than we can imagine, not worse, not less. Our guesses may be silly, but that's not because they're too strong, too much, but because they're too weak, too little.

Sal: It sounds great. I can't wait.

Chris: It can begin now, you know.

Heaven begins now.

Sal: What?

Chris: The life of Heaven. We didn't even mention the best thing about it. That's knowing and loving God intimately, sharing in his very own life. And that begins the moment you believe in him and accept him.

Sal: I don't see anything as exalted and wonderful as Heaven on earth, even in you.

Chris: It's only a seed, but it's there. It takes time to grow. It may be invisible, underground, like a seed that didn't come up yet. But it's there.

Sal: Like the unborn baby who's already in the world but doesn't see it until birth?

Chris: Yes.

Sal: So we're all in Heaven already, but we don't see it until after death?

Chris: Not everybody, not automatically. It takes a free choice. It's like getting pregnant. God doesn't plant his seed in you unless you let him. He's a gentleman. He doesn't force you.

Sal: So there is an alternative?—spiritual barrenness as well as spiritual pregnancy?

Chris: Yes. It's called Hell. Let's talk about that next time.

Sal: Must we?

Chris: Yes.

Sal: Why?

Chris: Because it's there. Because it's true. Like a hole in the ice: you need to put up signs to warn people away.

Sal: O.K., next time.

Dialogue Fourteen

Hell

Sal: All right, Chris. Today's the day you try to defend the indefensible.

Chris: What do you mean?

Sal: You promised to talk about Hell today.

Chris: Yes.

Sal: Well, of all the teachings of Christianity, Hell is certainly the most indefensible. It's just terrible!

Chris: Yes, it is. But just because a thing is terrible, that doesn't mean it isn't real. Terrible pains exist. Death exists. Concentration camps exist. You can't just refuse to believe in it because it's terrible.

Sal: That's true. That would be wishful thinking. But don't you wish you didn't have to believe in Hell?

Chris: Of course. Do you think I want there to be a Hell?

Sal: No, but apparently your God does. That's my objection: How can this loving God of yours create a Hell?

Chris: I don't think he did. I think we do.

Sal: You mean Hell isn't real, just in our imagination?

Chris: No, it's real, just as sin is real. But *we* create it, not God, just as we create sin, God doesn't.   *We create Hell.*

Sal: Is Hell a real place?

131

Chris: I don't know whether it's a physical place. Maybe it's more like a state of mind. Like a nightmare. But a real state of mind.

Sal: So then Heaven would be a state of mind too?

Chris: Certainly not. Heaven is a real place.

Sal: Then Heaven and Hell aren't parallel, equivalent.

Chris: No more than good and evil are. Evil is bent good, perverted good. Like a parasite on the good.

Sal: So why could Hell be a state of mind and Heaven not?

Chris: Because every state of mind, shut up in itself, is eventually hellish, and because every objective reality is ultimately heavenly. Objective reality is either God the Creator or something he created. That's what we need: contact with God and God's creation. I think in Hell we lose that contact and we're all shut up within ourselves, our own nightmares. We don't care about or love or enjoy anything real, anything objective, anything outside ourselves. I think Hell is pure egotism.

Sal: That sounds much worse than fire and brimstone.

Chris: Yes. You might escape the fire and brimstone, but you never escape yourself.

Sal: Do you escape yourself in Heaven?

Chris: In a sense. You forget yourself in Heaven. God is so beautiful that you're thinking of him all the time. That's why it's so joyful.

Joy is self-forgetful. *Sal:* Joy is forgetting yourself, then?

Chris: All joy is self-forgetful. Think of the most joyful time you ever had. Were you thinking about yourself, or did you "lose yourself" in it?

Sal: I forgot myself. You're right. Turning around to look at myself would have spoiled it.

Chris: That's the difference between Heaven and Hell, I think. In Heaven God is so perfectly present and so perfectly seen that everyone is self-forgetfully enjoying him, head over heels in love with him.

Sal: I see. It's when you love someone most that you forget the most about yourself.

Chris: And that's also when you're the happiest. People who are unhappiest—like suicides—are always thinking about themselves.

Sal: Aren't we supposed to be thinking about our consciences, our sins?

Chris: Only to repent and confess and then to forget. If we keep thinking about how well we're doing, we won't do well. And we'll get into the trap of thinking one of three unhappy thoughts: either we'll think we're doing really well, and start feeling proud and self-satisfied and self-righteous, or we'll think we're doing badly and start feeling depressed and self-hating and despairing, or we'll think we're not particularly good *or* bad, and start feeling bored and wishy-washy.

Sal: What's the way out? Those sound like the only three alternatives.

Chris: To stop thinking about ourselves so much. To forget ourselves and think about God and other people instead. That's heavenly.

Sal: I see. That certainly makes Heaven and Hell relevant to life here and now. Well, here's another question for you. Even if God doesn't create a place called Hell, even if we make our own Hell, doesn't God send people there? If he's so loving, why doesn't he take everybody to Heaven?

Chris: He doesn't put anyone in Hell against their will. Heaven's doors are open to everyone. It's up to us.

Sal: I thought Heaven was only for good people.

Chris: Wrong. If that were so, it would be empty. There's sin in all of us, and the best people are the first to admit it. There are only two kinds of people:

Does God condemn people to Hell?

sinners who think they're saints and saints who know they're sinners.

Sal: So who makes it to Heaven and who goes to Hell?

Chris: That's such an important question—the most important question anyone can possibly ask—that we've got to save another day for it, all right? Tomorrow we'll talk about roads to Heaven and Hell. But today let's finish talking about Hell.

Sal: O.K. Let's see, what have we come up with so far? We make Hell, not God; it's a state of our own soul, not a material place; and we have to choose to go there by our own free choice, right?

Chris: Right.

Sal: Then why would anyone ever choose Hell instead of Heaven? It must be underpopulated.

Chris: No one knows the population statistics except God.

Sal: But why would any prefer misery to joy?

Chris: For the same reason they do now: they get their own way in Hell. In Hell everyone says, "*My* will be done." In Heaven everyone says to God, "Thy will be done." In Hell they all sing, "I did it my way." In Heaven they sing, "God's way is the best way."

Sal: Sounds like Hell is a lot like earth.

Chris: Exactly. Relevance again. In Hell they all do what a lot of people want to do on earth: create their own values.

Sal: What's the difference between earth and Hell then?

Chris: After death, God's creation is gone; the world is gone; your body is gone. You have only what you wanted in the depths of your soul. If you wanted to be your own God, you couldn't do that while you were in God's world. But you can once the world is gone.

Sal: So everyone eventually gets just what he wants.

Chris: Yes. Fair, isn't it?

Sal: Yes. Is that God's justice?

Chris: Yes.

Sal: I thought God's justice was like keeping a list of rules and being punished each time we broke a rule.

Chris: That's not wholly false, but it's a child's version of the truth. The rules are there for a reason. They tell us how to be heavenly instead of hellish right now. Every choice we make is one or the other. Every choice changes us a little bit, makes us a little better or a little worse, a little more heavenly or a little more hellish.

Sal: That's why God is so concerned about our behavior?

Chris: He's concerned about *us*. He doesn't want just right *behavior*. He could get that from a robot, or a puppet. He wants what a lover wants: our hearts, our selves.

Sal: And our happiness?

Chris: Yes. Following God's law is the road to happiness. God wants us to avoid sin for the same reason you want the person you love to avoid suicide or addiction or anything else that's harmful. You love them. The more you love someone the more you care about who he is, and what he's making himself into, what kind of person.

Sal: I still don't understand why God doesn't just take us all to Heaven now if he loves us so much.

Chris: Against our will, or with it?

Sal: With it.

Chris: Suppose we won't.

Sal: Against it, then.

Chris: But then it wouldn't make us happy. It would be like an opera fan being taken to a rock concert or a

We get what we want.

God wants our hearts.

rock fan being taken to an opera. If you don't want it, you won't enjoy it if you get it.

Sal: So if God took everybody out of Hell and put them in Heaven, they wouldn't enjoy it?

Chris: Right. In fact, maybe Hell and Heaven are the same thing: God's own truth and goodness, loved and enjoyed by the people in Heaven and hated and feared by the people in Hell. Maybe the fires of Hell are really the light of God. Like two people at a concert: for one it's heavenly music, for another it's hellish noise.

Sal: Why do you think it's *light*?

Chris: Light is a symbol for truth. Some people prefer lies and deception and sneaking, and when their lies are exposed they don't repent and accept the truth and live in the truth, but instead they hate it and try to hide from it with more lies. That's practicing a little bit of the life of Hell on earth.

Sal: And being honest is practicing Heaven's life on earth?

Chris: Yes.

Why do we have free will? *Sal:* Well, here's another question, then. If it's our own free will that chooses Hell, why did God make us with free will in the first place? If we had no freedom to choose Hell, nobody would ever go there.

Chris: Right, but then we'd be like machines, not people. When you ask why God created us with free will you're asking why God made people instead of machines, why he made us at all.

Sal: Well, why *did* he?

Chris: Aren't you glad he did?

Sal: Of course . . .

Chris: Not "of course". Not everybody is. Some people resent being born.

Sal: How awful! But why did he?

Chris: Because he loved us.

Sal: But before he created us we weren't there to love.

Chris: He loved us into existence. Like an artist who loves the work of art even before it's made. Like parents having babies, loving them into existence, loving them before they exist.

Sal: Oh. I just thought of something. Is that why sex is so important? It's like what God does?

Chris: Yes. It's sacred because it creates life. Some other day we should talk more about that too.

Sal: Back to Hell for a minute. You've answered my objections to it, but why do you believe it in the first place? Why does there have to be a Hell at all?

Chris: There doesn't. It's up to us. We create it.

Sal: I mean, why do you believe in it?

Chris: For the same reason I believe in Heaven: Jesus says so.

Sal: Didn't Jesus talk all about love and justice and compassion? Wasn't it Saint Paul or the early Church that changed Jesus' message of love into a message of fear and started talking more about sin and Hell?

Chris: Not at all. Read the New Testament and you'll see for yourself. No one ever talked more about sin and Hell than Jesus did.

Jesus talked about Hell.

Sal: Gentle Jesus? Kindly Jesus? Compassionate Jesus?

Chris: That's half of Jesus. Jesus is also strong and fearsome. You don't crucify someone who's only gentle.

Sal: How can he be both? How can he be compassionate if he talks so much about Hell?

Chris: As a doctor is compassionate if he warns you a lot against a disease that's life threatening. He does it because he loves you. He does everything he can to keep you safe. He even appeals to fear if it's necessary.

Sal: I see. So your belief in Hell comes down to Jesus too. Just like everything else you believe.

Chris: Yes, as I told you. It all hangs together. And the point of it all is Jesus.

Sal: How is Jesus the point of Hell?

Chris: First, he tells us it exists and warns us against it. Second, he saves us from it. And that's the crucial thing. He's like a doctor: first he diagnoses our disease, and then he offers a healing. The healing is the crucial thing.

Sal: And what's that?

Chris: It's called "salvation".

Sal: And what do we have to do to get that?

Chris: That's the great question: "What must I do to be saved?" We'll talk about that next time.

Dialogue Fifteen

Roads to Heaven and Hell

Sal: All right, Chris, let's talk about the question you said yesterday was the most important question in the world. How do we get to Heaven? "What must I do to be saved?" I wonder if it isn't like the joke about the Vermont farmer giving directions to the city slicker who's lost: "You can't get there from here." Heaven and Hell seem so far away that it seems like arrogant nonsense for us to talk about roads from here to there. What do we know about it anyway?

Chris: Not much. That's why we need God to tell us the way. It *is* far away—farther than any rocket ship could ever go. Heaven isn't part of our physical universe. In another sense, it's very close: it's where God is, and God is here too. It's the seed that God plants in your soul right here and now. It begins now.

Sal: I'm confused. Is it a state of mind in our own souls or is it a real place?

Chris: Heaven is both. Perhaps Hell is only a state of mind. But it's *real.*

Sal: But Heaven *is* a real *place*?

Chris: Yes. That's why some roads can lead to it and others away from it.

Sal: You don't mean physical roads, or rocket ship lanes.

Chris: No, spiritual roads. They're just as real as bodily roads, you know. And they really lead to really different destinations. That's why the most important thing in the world is to be sure you're on the right road.

Sincerity isn't enough. *Sal:* But won't you go to Heaven as long as you're sincere?

Chris: No.

Sal: How do you know you won't?

Chris: How do you know you will?

Sal: That's how I would arrange it if I were God.

Chris: But are you?

Sal: No . . .

Chris: Well, God has told us how he has arranged it. And it's not that way. He provided a road. His name is Jesus.

Sal: I thought Jesus said "Seek and you shall find."

Chris: He did.

Sal: Doesn't that mean that anybody who's sincere will be saved?

Chris: It means that anybody who sincerely seeks *God* will be saved.

Sal: So the seeking is all we need.

Chris: No. We need finding too. We need two things: seeking *and* finding.

Sal: But if we seek, we'll find.

Chris: Yes.

Sal: So if we're sincerely seeking God and God's way to Heaven . . .

Chris: Then we'll find Jesus. Because Jesus is God's way. You see, you have to find the real road, the real way. It's objective, not subjective. All the sincerity in the world isn't enough by itself. You can't get to the

Pacific Ocean by sincerely walking east from here. It's the wrong road.

Sal: That seems awfully hard-nosed.

Chris: Reality is hard-nosed. We have to learn to live in it. We can't pretend we can get to the Pacific by walking east, or to Heaven by ignoring Jesus.

Sal: I can't believe Jesus is the only way.

Chris: Why not?

Sal: God is just, right?

Chris: Right. More than just, but not less.

Sal: Then God wouldn't let anyone go to Hell instead of Heaven unless they deserved it, right?

Chris: Right.

Sal: And if you're sincere, you deserve to go to Heaven.

Chris: That's what you say. That's not what God said.

Sal: My way seems kinder and juster than your way.

Chris: Not my way; God's way.

Sal: What you say God's way is.

Chris: How can you tell that your way is better? You haven't looked at God's way yet.

Sal: My way seems reasonable.

Chris: I think not. For one thing, where's your cutoff point? *How* sincere do you have to be to make it to Heaven? Sincerity is a matter of degree; Heaven and Hell are not. Would you make Heaven dependent on whether you attained 49.9% sincerity or 50% sincerity? Is *that* just?

Sal: That is a problem, I guess. Maybe I should look at God's alternative first. Mine seems to have some problems.

Chris: I think you'd better! What right do we have to tell God how to run things, anyway? That would be like a bug telling us how to run human life.

Is Jesus the only way?

Sal: We have to get the road map from God, then?

Chris: Yes. When you go to your friend's house and you've never been there before, who do you get directions from? Yourself or your friend?

Sal: My friend.

Chris: Why?

Sal: Because the one who lives there should know what roads lead there.

Chris: Exactly. And Heaven is where God lives. So we'd better ask *him* what the road to Heaven is.

Finding God on our own

Sal: So all the people in the world who are trying to find God can't find him unless he tells them the way?

Chris: That's right.

Sal: I'm not convinced of that. Why can't we find him by our own reason?

Chris: Reason itself tells you that won't work.

Sal: How?

Chris: If you're trying to know something passive, like a rock, you do all the work, you go to it. The rock just lies there, right?

Sal: Right.

Chris: Now take it one step higher: knowing a person. If the other person doesn't want to let you get to know him, you never will. You have to win his free choice. The action is evenly divided. Both of you are active. It takes two to make friends.

Sal: Right.

Chris: Now when you want to know God, all the activity, all the initiative has to come from him. For us to know God is like a toddler knowing a parent: the parent has to teach the toddler.

Sal: O.K. You've given good reasons for listening to God. What does God say? What's his answer to my question?

Chris: The question is: What's the road to Heaven? And the answer is Jesus again. The One who said, "I am the way . . . no one comes to the Father except by me."

Sal: How does that work? How does Jesus take you to Heaven?

Chris: You don't have to know how a plane works to use it, do you? All you have to do is get in and trust it to bring you to where you want to go.

Sal: And Jesus is God's plane to Heaven?

Chris: Sort of. All you have to do is get in him and trust him to take you there.

Sal: And God's air force has only one plane?

Chris: That's what he said, yes.

Sal: So all the people in the world except Christians are going to Hell?

Chris: I never said that.

Sal: What about all the people who believe other religions then?

Chris: Let's talk about them next time. Let's talk about us now. Let's not let ourselves be distracted from the "one thing necessary".

Sal: All right. So what do you mean by getting in Jesus, like a plane? It's a symbol, not literal. What does it symbolize?

Chris: The two doors that lead into the plane are: "repent" and "believe". You have to go through both of them to get in.

Sal: What does that mean? Repent means feel sorry for my sins, right?   *Repentance*

Chris: No, repentance is more than a feeling. Feelings come and go. Repentance is an act of will. It means turning around, facing God instead of running away from him. Like the Prodigal Son in the parable coming home to his father. Saying "yes" to God instead of "no". Saying to God, "I need you. I'm a sinner and I can't save myself. I want to do it your way instead of my way."

Sal: But after you repent you still sin again.

Chris: But you don't *want* to sin again. You don't *will* sin, you will God. And when you sin, you're honestly sorry.

Faith *Sal:* What's the other door? What is it to "believe"? How much do you have to believe? Everything in the Bible? What's the cutoff point there?

Chris: Wrong question. It's not a question of a cutoff point on an exam, getting a passing grade in theology or ethics. God doesn't send you to Hell for a 59 instead of a 60.

Sal: If my question is the wrong question, what's the right one?

Chris: Not how *much* you have to believe but *what* you have to believe; and not *what* but *who*.

Sal: So faith alone saves you?

Chris: Yes.

Sal: What about good works?

Chris: They're the fruit of faith. Faith alone saves you because it isn't just intellectual faith; it's a faith that includes hope and love that always results in good works, just as a plant's roots result in its leaves.

Sal: What do you mean by "intellectual faith"?

Chris: Faith in the teaching.

Sal: Why can't that save you?

Chris: Even the Devil has that. The Bible says, "Do you believe that there's one God? Big deal! The devils also believe that, and shake with fear."

Sal: So we have to do good works too.

Chris: We do. But they don't save us. Jesus saves us. We don't do good works to be saved, we do good works because we've *been* saved.

Sal: But they're part of the salvation package?

Chris: Yes. As fruit is part of the plant package. The Bible says that faith without works is dead. Works are a proof that faith is alive.

Sal: Don't Catholics and Protestants disagree about that?

Chris: They seem to; at least each *emphasizes* a different thing. Protestants emphasize that faith alone saves us, and Catholics emphasize that we must do good works too.

Sal: That sounds to me like one emphasizing the roots and the other the fruits of the same plant.

Chris: Well, it's true that Protestants admit we must obey God and do the works he commands us to do, and Catholics admit that we're saved by God's grace, not by our deeds alone.

Sal: One more question, if you don't mind.

Chris: Go ahead.

Sal: How does salvation work? It seems so arbitrary. If I said to you, "I'll give you incredible happiness if only you believe I'm from Mars", wouldn't that seem silly?

Chris: Yes.

Sal: Isn't that like what Jesus says? "I'll give you eternal life with God in Heaven if only you believe I'm the Savior?"

Chris: No, it's different.

Sal: How?

Chris: In two ways. First, the object of faith isn't a teaching about him but him, not a doctrine but a person. Second, faith isn't just intellectual belief but more like accepting a marriage proposal: it's actually allowing Christ to come in to your soul and make it spiritually pregnant. It's not just a change in your attitude toward him, but a change in the real relationship between you. He really comes in.

Sal: So Christianity is sort of like being haunted, or demon-possessed? But by a good spirit instead of a bad one?

Chris: Yes! It's real, not just mental. When you ask him to come in, he really does. It's not just a nice idea.

Being born again   *Sal:* And is that "being born again"?

Chris: Yes. That's another word for it. It means getting a new nature, just as you do when you're born, or when you get pregnant. Our soul is barren soil until God deposits the seed of his own life in it, and he doesn't do that until we let him. That's what faith is: letting him give us himself, his own life. That's why faith is necessary for salvation: because faith opens the door of the soul to Jesus the Savior.

Sal: Why does he limit that gift only to those who believe in him?

Chris: Not because he's stingy. But because he wants your free trust and love. He made you free and he sticks to that. It's up to you. He's done his part. He even died to save you.

Sal: How does that work? Why does Jesus have to die?

Chris: Some other time we'll take a whole conversation on that. But the point we shouldn't let ourselves be distracted from today is this: he did his part, however that works. He's always ready. Now it's up to us. And whenever you're ready, it will happen. You'll be saved.

Sal: You mean it can really happen any minute?

Chris: Whenever you want it. Right now, if you will.

Sal: That sounds terribly dramatic.

Chris: Life *is* terribly dramatic. We're poised on the razor's edge of Heaven or Hell.

Sal: Every moment?

Chris: Can you die at any moment, or not?

Sal: You can.

Chris: Then it's at every moment. The thing separating us from eternity is a tiny, thin membrane. If you were to die today, where would you be?

Sal: I don't know.

Chris: Don't you think you should?

Dialogue Sixteen

Other Religions

Sal: Chris, here's an objection to Christianity that I didn't think of before. It really bothers me.

Chris: Then it really bothers me too. Let's take a look at it.

Sal: There's one big thing wrong with the Christian religion.

Chris: What's that?

Sal: That it's a religion.

Chris: You mean you have something against all religion?

Sal: No, I mean Christianity is only one religion among many. It just feels provincial to claim it's the only true one. Every other religion claims that too.

Chris: I think I understand how you feel. It seems unlikely that just one political system, or one philosophy, or one art, or one economic system, is the right one. There's something good in all of them. So you think the same is true of religions.

Sal: Exactly. The world is a big place. Christianity isn't everything.

Chris: If Christianity were just another religion, I'd see your point. But Christianity is Christ.

Sal: We always get back to him, don't we?

Chris: Yes. No other religious teacher ever claimed to be God. His claim is unique. Christianity is unique because Christ is unique.

Is Christianity just another religion?

Sal: Christianity still seems small, particular, one among many.

Chris: If Christ is God, he's bigger than the whole universe. Christ isn't small. He made the galaxies!

Christ on other
planets
Sal: Oh! Do you think he visited other planets just as he visited this one?

Chris: Why not? If there are extraterrestrial beings on other planets, they're his creatures too.

Sal: With ten arms and three eyes and green rubber skin?

Chris: Why not?

Sal: I thought only we were created in the image of God.

Chris: We are, but the Bible never said *only* us.

Sal: But if we're made in God's image, how can E.T. be made in God's image?

Chris: God is spirit. The image of God in us is the soul, not the body. E.T. would have a soul too, however different his body is.

Sal: So E.T. is made in God's image too?

Chris: Of course. If E.T.s exist.

Sal: And do you think Christ became an E.T. on E.T.'s home planet?

Chris: Why not? Especially if they needed him as we did, if they fell into sin and needed a Savior.

Sal: You mean maybe some planets didn't sin?

Chris: Maybe. We didn't *have* to sin, you know. That's why we're rightly blamed for it. That much is certain, however you interpret the Garden of Eden story. Sin was our fault, our free choice.

Sal: So maybe E.T. people didn't sin, and then Christ didn't have to come to E.T.'s planet.

Chris: Maybe. But maybe he came anyway, not to die but just to say hello.

Sal: I guess if there was no sin, he wouldn't die because nobody would want to kill him.

Chris: Right.

Sal: You know, I never thought of Christ on other planets.

Chris: That's because you had too small a view of Christ. That's why you had that objection to Christianity.

Sal: But what about the other religions on earth? Let's get back to earth. The fact remains there are other religions and they all claim to be true.

Chris: That's so, but you're looking at it in a mistaken perspective. Christianity isn't a product in the religious supermarket of the world. You don't come in and pick whichever religion you like best, like fruit or meats.

Sal: Why not? Christianity *is* a religion, isn't it?

Chris: The New Testament never calls it that. In fact, it never uses the word "Christianity" at all. It talks about Christ.

Sal: Are you saying I should believe in Christ but not Christianity?

Chris: No, I'm saying that Christianity *means* believing in Christ. Christianity doesn't mean believing in Christianity. We don't have faith in faith; we have faith in Christ.

Christ or Christianity?

Sal: We keep getting back to him all the time.

Chris: Yes, in every conversation, no matter what point we start from. This time from the starting point of Christianity.

Sal: But Christianity is also a whole bunch of teachings, and some of those contradict the teachings of other religions.

Chris: It *has* teachings, yes. Just as you *have* two arms. And some of them contradict other religions, yes. So what? Did you expect all religions to teach the same things?

Sal: No, but there's something in everything, some truth in every one.

Chris: That's no news. What's news is that there's everything in something.

Sal: You mean all truth is in Christianity?

Chris: I mean all truth is in Jesus himself. Jesus makes Christianity unique. No other religious teacher claims to be God incarnate. Not Moses, not Mohammed, not Buddha, not Confucius, not Lao-Tzu, not Zoroaster. Only Jesus.

Sal: But aren't there unique Christian teachings too?

Chris: Yes. But they're not the main reason to be a Christian. Christ is. Even if *you* don't believe that all the Christian teachings are true, there stands Christ, the unique Savior, the only man who claimed to be God, and claims your whole life as his own, your life in time and your life in eternity. Let's not forget that one simple point as we talk about other things. Let's not forget the center.

Sal: O.K. But I'm curious about the teachings of other religions. How different are they from Christianity?

Ethical teachings   *Chris:* Their *ethical* teachings are usually very similar, because everyone in the world has a conscience and knows that things like selfishness and hatred and injustice and lying and cheating and cowardice and stealing and murder and adultery are wrong, and that unselfishness and love and justice and truth and honesty and courage and respect for property and life and sex are right. Jesus may be the *greatest* ethical teacher, but he didn't teach a brand *new* ethics.

Sal: So if the difference isn't in ethics, where is it?

Chris: Besides the main difference, Jesus himself?

Sal: Yes. I'm not forgetting that.

Chris: In theology, in the beliefs about God.

Sal: What do other religions believe about God?

Chris: Christianity believes that God is one and personal: a person, an *I*. So do Jews and Moslems. All other people believe either in atheism (that's no god) or polytheism (that's many gods) or pantheism (that's an impersonal god).

Sal: Polytheism—that's paganism, right? Like in the myths?

Chris: Yes. Most primitive religions are polytheistic. "Poly" means "many".

Sal: What's pantheism?

Chris: Pantheism believes God is everything. "Pan" means "everything". Everything is part of God, according to them; God never created a world distinct from himself. He's not a person; he doesn't know you or love you. You can't pray to him. He's just a force, a "cosmic consciousness", and there's nothing else outside of him. Really, we should say "it" instead of "him".

Sal: What religions are pantheistic?

Chris: Most forms of Hinduism and Buddhism, and I think Taoism.

Sal: It's Oriental.

Chris: Yes, but becoming more popular in the West lately.

Sal: And Jews and Moslems are theists too?

Chris: Yes. They worship the same God we do.

Sal: I thought Moslems call him "Allah".

Chris: A God by any other name would smell as sweet. They learned about God from the Jews, just as we Christians did. All three religions accept what we call the Old Testament. Christians add the New Testament, and Moslems add the Koran, which Mohammed wrote.

Sal: But only Christians believe Christ is God incarnate?

Chris: Right.

Sal: And only Christians believe God is three Persons, right? The Trinity?

Chris: Right.

Sal: Isn't that a contradiction?

Chris: No, because God isn't three gods and one God, not three natures and one nature, not three persons and one person. He's three persons in one nature, one God. Some other time we must go into Christian theology as taught by the creeds.

Sal: Let's get back to comparative religions.

Chris: You know, one writer described comparative religion as "a way of being comparatively religious".

Sal: He thought it was an escape from believing in any one of them?

Chris: Yes. It *could* be misused that way.

Sal: Do you think we shouldn't study other religions, then?

Chris: No, I think we should look at everything, search for truth everywhere. All truth is God's truth.

Sal: Do you think I'll find any truth in other religions?

Chris: Certainly. There's some truth everywhere, something to learn from everyone. I think there's a lot of profound wisdom in other religions. And also some profound errors. But no other Christ.

Pagan mythology   *Sal:* Do you think there's truth even in pagan mythology?

Chris: Yes. Don't those stories sometimes move you deeply and mysteriously? Psychologists have found a lot of truth about our unconscious mind through studying the myths. And they contain a lot of good guesses, or good dreams that are fulfilled in Christianity—like the story of the dying and rising God.

Sal: That's in paganism too?

Chris: Yes, but only in the myths, not in history. Their gods weren't historical figures, with dates and places and eyewitnesses who knew them and lived with them, like Jesus.

Sal: The stories are just dreams, then.

Chris: Yes, but some of them are good dreams, maybe even dreams from God messed up and misunderstood. The Bible says that God revealed himself to the whole human race, you know, not just to Jews and Christians. Maybe these stories that keep cropping up in many different cultures are one way he revealed himself: stories about a creation and a fall and a flood and a law and a savior-god. A Christian doesn't have to reject everything in pagan religions.

Sal: How else did God reveal himself to the pagans?

Chris: Through nature and conscience.

Sal: What do you mean, through nature?

Chris: Medieval Christians put it this way: God wrote two books, nature and Scripture. Nature teaches you a bit about God. Remember the argument from cause and effect? And the argument from design? Even good pagans like Plato and Aristotle knew there was one supreme God of some sort just by reasoning about nature, trying to explain nature.

Sal: And what about conscience?

Chris: That's the universal ethics, that worldwide sense of morality that we were talking about before. We all know what we ought to do, in general, even though no one does it perfectly.

Sal: So what are the other differences between Christianity and other religions?

Chris: That's too big a question to answer quickly. There are two kinds of differences, to start with. Some are just *differences*, like the differences between cats and dogs, that don't amount to contradiction, so that

Nature and conscience

you can believe or use both. Others are *contradictions,* like one God versus many gods.

Sal: What about Buddhist meditation? Is that different or contradictory to Christianity? Can a Christian use Zen?

Chris: Christians differ about that. Christ never told us about other religions, just as he never told us whether there was evolution or not. Christians who disagree about those things can still agree about Christ and everything he taught.

Sal: But what about all the differences that *do* amount to contradictions? Don't you have to believe that Christianity is right and everybody else wrong about those things?

Chris: Of course.

Sal: That seems pretty arrogant.

Chris: It's God's Word, not mine. I'm just repeating what he told us. I'm the mail carrier, not the letter writer. God's the letter writer.

Sal: Doesn't every religion claim to be a message from God or the gods?

Chris: Yes, but only Christianity knows the messenger, Christ.

Sal: So only you Christians have the message from God straight and direct?

Chris: It's for everybody, not just us. That's why we send missionaries all over the world.

Sal: That's another thing that bothers me. What right do you have to ask a good Hindu or Buddhist to convert to Christianity?

Conversion *Chris:* To convert to *Christ.* Christ commanded us to "go into all the world and preach the good news."

Sal: Then it's *his* claim that's arrogant. Didn't he say "No one can come to the Father except by me"?

Chris: Yes. If that's not true, then it certainly is arrogant. And blasphemous. But not if it's true.

Sal: "Come to the Father" means "be saved", "go to Heaven", doesn't it?

Chris: Yes.

Sal: So Jews and Hindus and everyone else go to Hell?

Chris: I didn't say that.

Sal: Do you think that?

Chris: No.

Sal: How could they go to Heaven if they don't know Christ?

Chris: I'm not sure they can't know Christ. I *am* sure God is just and fair, and gives everyone a chance to be saved somehow.

Sal: O.K., but how? Jesus says he's the only way.

Chris: Yes. There's no other way. Jesus isn't one among many men who raised himself up to God, but the one and only God who lowered himself to us. So somehow God must give everyone a chance to know Jesus.

Sal: How?

Chris: I don't know. Maybe at the moment of death. Or maybe in an unconscious way during this life. Maybe when someone seeks truth for its own sake and goodness for its own sake, he's really seeking the way to God even though he doesn't know that Jesus is the way. So when he meets him at death, he'll recognize him as the one he was always seeking in the depths of his soul. Paul told the pagan Greeks in Athens that he was going to preach to them about "the Unknown God" they were *already worshipping* in ignorance.

Sal: That sounds like the loving God of Jesus.

Chris: I think so too. If God loves us so much that he comes to earth to die for us, I think he loves us enough to find a way to allow pagans to choose to be saved too.

Are non-Christians saved?

Sal: I couldn't worship a God who would send half the world to Hell for no fault of their own.

Chris: Oh, it's through our own fault, all right. None of us *deserves* Heaven. It's pure grace. If God hadn't sent Jesus to save us, he wouldn't have been unfair. Jesus is a gift, not what we deserve.

Sal: I think I'm getting to like this God of yours, Chris. Maybe even to love him.

Chris: That's what's going to make you a Christian, Sal, more than any of my arguments.

Dialogue Seventeen

Relevance

Sal: Chris, I have a doubt about everything we've talked about so far.

Chris: A doubt about *everything*? How can that be? Doubts are always about *something*, aren't they? Something in particular?

Sal: This doubt isn't about whether Christianity is *true*, but about whether it's *relevant*. Isn't all this talk about religion an escape from life?

Chris: We haven't been talking about religion. We've been talking about Jesus.

Sal: Jesus, then. What difference does it make, really, if you believe in Jesus or not?

What difference does Jesus make?

Chris: That's a legitimate question, Sal. If something makes no difference, then let's forget it. It's just not important.

Sal: So you agree with my demand to make Christianity relevant?

Chris: No, I agree with your question, "*Is* Christianity relevant?" We don't have to change Christianity or even add anything to it to make it relevant. It *is* relevant. It does make a difference. It doesn't need something new to do that; it's been doing that for nearly two thousand years.

Sal: How? What good will it do for me?

Chris: Don't you remember what you said when we began these conversations? You said the first question, if you're honest, is not what good it will do for you but whether it's true or not. You don't want to believe a lie, do you? Not even if it will do you good.

Sal: No. I agree it has to be true. But it also has to be good for me. Don't you agree?

Chris: Yes, but watch out you don't make it a means to your own ends. Truth isn't a means, Christianity isn't a means, above all Christ isn't a means to some other end, like ending wars or giving you good feelings. Christ is God. Christianity is loving and trusting and serving Christ. *He's* the end.

Sal: Christ again. You keep turning everything back to Christ himself.

Chris: For good reason. You see, if we just spoke about Christianity and not about Christ, we might think it was to make Christianity a means to something else as our end. But you can't do that with Christ. Christianity isn't God. But Christ is God. And God can't be anything less than the absolute, the ultimate end, the One everything is for.

Sal: I thought God was the beginning, the source, the creator of everything.

Chris: Yes, and also the final end of everything.

Sal: O.K. So Christ is not a means to my ends. But my question remains: What difference does he make to me here and how? I see the difference he makes in Heaven, in eternity. But what about right now?

Chris: That's a good question, a strong question. And there are good answers, strong answers.

Sal: I hope you're going to get your answers from experience, not just theory.

How Christians changed the world

Chris: I do. From looking at myself and my life with and without Christ and comparing them. From looking at other people's lives before and after believing in Christ. From looking at the history of the Christian Church to see what difference it made to the world. From looking at the difference Christ himself made to the lives of his disciples in the Gospels. From asking how twelve Jewish fishermen and peasants turned the world upside down.

Sal: Good question. How did they?

Chris: What do you think?

Sal: Well, I don't think it could have been the Christian theology. It's not obvious, not easy to believe.

Chris: No, it wasn't just their theology that won the world, though Christians found it did make sense, and reason was on their side.

Sal: Their love, then, right?

Chris: Jesus' love. They told it and they showed it. The world sat up and took notice when it saw Jesus' disciples, just as it noticed Jesus, because it saw Jesus living in them and acting through them. The world met Christ through Christians. His Spirit was in them. The world saw a kind of love it had never seen before, and it said, "Look how those Christians love one another!" *Christ the lover*

Sal: How was it a different kind of love?

Chris: It was unselfish love instead of selfish love. It was self-forgetful love instead of self-regarding, self-conscious love. It was love extended to everyone instead of love limited to social class or race or sex. It was love of the concrete individual, the neighbor, not love of "humanity" in some safe, vague, general way. It was genuine, and people respect the genuine. There's so much around that's fake.

Sal: I can see how that would win the world. Do you think that's why Christianity lost half the modern world? Because Christians didn't love as Christ did?

Chris: Yes, that's exactly how I think it happened. And I think we can win the world back again in exactly the same way.

Sal: "Everybody loves a lover", right?

Chris: Right.

Sal: Anything else that makes Christianity relevant?

Chris: Isn't that enough?

Sal: Yes, but I suspect there's more too.

Christ the meaning   *Chris:* You're right. Here's another thing. Christ gives me a *meaning* for my life. I know my life is part of God's design and plan and Providence. It's not just an empty, meaningless jumble. It has order. God is the author, and the details of my life are connected like the details of a story. It all has meaning, even the parts I don't understand, because God knows it.

Sal: I guess that's necessary. If you think life is meaningless, there's no reason to keep going.

Chris: And if there's no God, or if God doesn't love me, then my life is like one of those little black boxes you buy in the joke shop: it makes funny noises when you turn it on, and lights blink on and off, and that's all, until the batteries wear out, and it dies.

Sal: Doesn't every religion give you a meaning? And some philosophies too?

Chris: Yes, but they're all abstract, sets of ideas. Christ is concrete. He makes God touchable, tangible, certain. He was right here!

Sal: Is there anything else?

Christ the goal   *Chris:* Yes, here's a third thing. Christ is my goal, my purpose as well as my author and designer; my end as well as my beginning. To work for him, to live for him, to love him, to hope for Heaven with him—it's my purpose for living, "a reason to live and a reason to die". How awful it would be not to have that, not to know what we're here for. No matter how rich you are, you're poor if you don't have a purpose to your life. And a lot of poor people and nations *are* really rich if they have this precious thing. That's why the suicide rate is so low in poor countries with strong religious faith and so high in rich countries with weak religious faith. If you have everything but God, you wake up one morning and ask yourself what your millions are all *for* and get no answer, and then there's nothing left to live for.

Sal: Is there anything else?

Chris: Yes, here's a fourth way Christianity is relevant: *Christ the life* death. My reason to live is also a reason to die. It makes death not just meaningless and fearful and the end of everything, but gives death meaning. Death brings me into the house of God.

Sal: You mean you don't fear death at all?

Chris: There's still a natural instinct to fear death, of course. Christians don't go around asking to be martyred. But when death comes we don't have to panic, because we know God the "good shepherd" leads us "through the valley of the shadow of death". We've got the biggie licked, the number one fear, the last enemy. Death was defeated by Christ on Easter Sunday. Death is like a bee without a sting now; the stinger is in Christ. That's why Paul taunts death and says, "O death, where is thy sting?"

Sal: I guess you answered my question, all right. I asked for one thing and I got four.

Chris: No, five. Here's one more. But it's harder to *Christ the joy* define. It's a sense—a sense of deep joy. Without Christ there may be a lot of temporary pleasures and superficial happiness, but never the deep joy and confidence that nothing in the world can separate us from God.

Sal: Does it overcome loneliness?

Chris: On the deepest level, yes, even though the *feeling* of loneliness sometimes is there, just as the instinctive fear of death is. But there's not the deep loneliness, because Christ is always with us. He promised that: "I am with you always, even till the end of the world." We're never alone. We're the family of Christ, the "body of Christ"; we have Christ and each other, our sisters and brothers, past and present—one very big and very close family. And here's another thing that gives us joy: a sense of adventure to life. Life on earth for a Christian is never dull, because its smallest details are part of a great, great story; they are steps on a road that lead to a great, great joy. You know how a great story makes even the ordinary things in it come alive with importance? Well, that's how we see life: a great story, a great adventure, the greatest adventure there is.

Sal: Sounds like a child's world. A big world.

Chris: Yes. "Unless you become as little children. . . ." We lost that sense of adventure, that sense of the bigness and importance of our life, when we "grew up". Christianity gives it back to us.

Sal: Isn't that childish?

Chris: No, childlike.

Sal: I mean, it's regression instead of progress.

Chris: No it isn't. Progress isn't just change; it's change for the better. A thing isn't better just because it's new, or worse just because it's old.

Sal: I guess not . . .

Chris: You don't seem convinced. Look here: Can we make mistakes, or not?

Sal: Of course we can.

Chris: And when we do, isn't the only way to progress to go back and correct the mistake?

Sal: Yes.

Chris: Well, it's not too late. God is the Father of the Prodigal Son. It's not too late to come home.

Dialogue Eighteen

Yes or No?

Sal: Chris, how come you understand Christianity so well? What's so special about you, anyway?

Chris: Nothing. Nothing at all, I assure you. I'm just like you.

Sal: Then how come you understand it better than I do?

Chris: God helps me. The Holy Spirit teaches me.

Sal: How do you know that? Do you have a private telephone line to Heaven or something?

Chris: No. I know that because God promised it. Promised it to anyone and everyone who believes. It's in the Bible.

Sal: Where?

Chris: The last few verses of the last book. Also Matthew 11 and a lot of other places. James says in his epistle something like this: "Do any of you need wisdom? Then let him ask God. God is generous, not stingy. God will give wisdom to anyone who asks for it. But he must ask in faith, believing."

Sal: Is that the key to understanding it? Believing it?

Chris: Yes. It says somewhere—Isaiah, I think—"Unless you believe, you will not understand".

Sal: I thought you had to understand a thing first before you believed in it.

Chris: A thing, maybe, but not a person. Remember? —It's a *person* I believe in: Jesus Christ. It works for persons the opposite way: you have to believe in them first, you have to trust them. That gets you inside them, so to speak. That's the only way you can really understand them.

Sal: I can't.

Chris: Can't what, Sal?

Sal: I just can't believe!

Chris: I know you can't, Sal. You're quite right about that. That's awfully honest and perceptive of you to see that.

Sal: But why? Why can't I believe?

Faith is a gift.   *Chris:* Because you don't have the grace of God. You need the grace of God to believe. Faith is a gift of God.

Sal: Do *you* have the grace of God, Chris?

Chris: Yes. That's how I can believe.

Sal: Why do you have it and I don't? What's so different about you? You said we *weren't* different.

Chris: Only one thing.

Sal: What's that?

Chris: I asked for it.

Sal: Is that all you have to do? Just ask for it?

Chris: Yes. But really—with your heart, not just your mouth.

Sal: And God promises I'll get it if I only ask?

Chris: Yes, "Seek and you shall find."

Sal: You mean my chances are 100%?

Chris: Exactly. 100%.

Sal: Oh!

Chris: Do you want it?

Sal: I think so.

Chris: Why do you hesitate?

Sal: Because it's scary. It's like getting married, only bigger.

Chris: Again you're very perceptive, Sal. Yes, saying "yes" or "no" to Jesus *is* like that.

Sal: Chris, does it have to be "yes" or "no" to Jesus?

Chris: More than that, Sal. It has to be all or nothing. *All or nothing*

Sal: Must you make it so black and white?

Chris: *He* did that, Sal. I'm just delivering his newspaper. He said, "He who is not for me is against me."

Sal: We've thought about a lot of things, you and I, in these conversations, and . . .

Chris: One thing, really. There's only "one thing necessary": himself.

Sal: But I have to know if it's true.

Chris: You have to *believe* that it's true, at least. Your honesty demands truth, however you get it, by reason or by faith.

Sal: Well, reason almost convinced me. You answered all my objections and you gave strong arguments for Christianity, but I don't think you proved it as you'd prove something in science. Doubts are still possible. It's not mathematically certain.

Chris: Of course. How could we be free otherwise? Christianity isn't like a scientific theory, it's like God's marriage proposal. Who proposes in mathematics?

Sal: If only I could be mathematically certain!

Chris: Do you think that would be *more* than faith?

Sal: Of course.

Chris: You're wrong. That would be less.

Sal: How is faith more?

Chris: Personal trust, for one thing. Like saying "yes" to a proposal. Hope, for another—hope in the future, when God will fulfill all his promises. Love, for a third thing. Faith includes love; proof doesn't. Faith is giving yourself. Losing yourself in God and finding yourself in God.

Sal: I don't have faith yet, and I don't have proof. How can I decide?

Chris: First, you can at least decide that you must decide.

Sal: What do you mean by that?

Chris: You can choose not to ignore the issue, not to be indifferent to it. You can choose to remember that one day—any day—you will die.

Agnosticism   *Sal:* Is that why you keep heading me away from agnosticism, away from a middle position between atheism and theism?

Chris: Yes.

Sal: But agnosticism seems the most honest position. I just don't know if Christianity is true or not. So I shouldn't choose one way or the other until I do.

Chris: You forget something: you're moving. You're on a ship called life sailing down a current called time. You want to get to your home port of Truth, and you can't make out with your binoculars whether the port you're looking at now, Christianity, is your home port or not.

Sal: That's my situation all right. I don't know whether to turn my ship around to head to that port, or turn it away.

Chris: But you must do one or the other. You can't just stay there hoping you'll see more clearly some day.

Sal: Why not? That's exactly what I think I'm doing.

Chris: Because you're moving. Time is carrying you nearer to the point of no return, death. One day all your fuel will run out and there will be no time left to get home. You have to turn home *before* then.

Sal: Oh!

Chris: To use another analogy, it's like that marriage proposal: you can say "wait a while" for a while, but not forever. Eventually the answer "wait" becomes "no".

Sal: You mean eventually God will have no more time for me? He'll get impatient and give up on me?

Chris: No. He never gives up on you. I mean you'll have no more time for *him*. The point of no return, remember?

Sal: So it has to be now, and it has to be "yes" or "no", eh?

Chris: Yes.

Sal: I can't decide. What can I do?

Chris: Think of your two options, your "yes" and your "no". That'll help you decide. What does each hold for you?

Sal: Each claims to hold the truth, but I don't know which one really does.

Chris: Reason can't decide for you?

Sal: No. Even though your arguments are very good, I don't think I can prove it's all true.

Chris: But you can't prove it's false either.

Sal: No.

Chris: Then you'll have to judge on some other basis.

Sal: What else is there if I don't have faith and I can't decide by reason?

Chris: You want happiness, don't you?

Sal: Yes.

Chris: Well, just look at which of your two options gives you any hope for that.

Sal: Let's see. Believing makes you happy because it gives you meaning. But not believing lets you be your own boss, your own God. I don't know which of those two is more important to me.

Chris: Oh, I don't mean just temporary, earthly happiness. What about infinite, eternal happiness? Which choice gives you that?

Sal: Christianity, if it's true. Neither one if it's false.

Chris: So your only chance is Christianity.

Sal: Let's see. What do I gain and what do I lose in each case? If Christianity is true and I believe, I lose nothing and gain everything, gain Heaven. But if it's true and I don't believe, I gain nothing but lose everything: I lose Heaven. And if it isn't true, I gain nothing and lose nothing, whether I believe or not. I see your point. But faith can't be just a gambler's calculation of odds.

Pascal's wager

Chris: No, it can't. But that can be a good argument *for* believing. You just discovered an argument Pascal discovered centuries ago. He called it his "wager". It's not faith, but it can move you in that direction, like a shove.

Sal: It's not enough.

Chris: One last try, then. It's "yes" or "no", remember? The alternative to "yes" is not "maybe" but "no". If you don't accept Jesus, you've rejected him.

Sal: There's still a gap ahead of me, like a canyon. I can't take "the leap of faith" across it yet.

Chris: You can, if you choose to. But there's a gap behind you too. You know too much. You can never return to innocence. If you don't go forward, you go back. If you don't say "yes", you say "no". Do you want to say "no" to God?

Sal: No. But that's an appeal to fear in him.

Chris: So? Fear can be reasonable and honest, if there's real danger.

Sal: I thought Christianity was supposed to be love.

Fear of the Lord

Chris: Love casts out fear, yes. But "the fear of the Lord is the beginning of wisdom." It's not the end, but it's the beginning. Both truths are important, and easily forgotten: that fear *is* the beginning, and that it's *not* the end. If God is your enemy instead of your friend, then you do well to fear him. If you refuse him, there really is something to fear in him.

Sal: Out with fear!

Chris: Then you'd better love him. That's the way to cast out fear.

Sal: Did *you* make that choice, Chris? Weren't you born a Christian? Did you have to go through the doubts I'm going through?

Chris: No one is born a Christian, Sal. We don't get faith from our parents, however much they help us. As one writer said, "God has no grandchildren". You have to make the choice yourself. It's the most responsible, most adult, most free, most personal choice you make in your life.

Sal: I see. I can't just ooze into Christ; I have to choose into Christ.

Chris: Why don't you talk to him about it?

Sal: You mean pray? How can I pray if I don't even know if God is real or not?

Chris: The way I suggested the other day. Just say, "God, I don't know if you exist or not. But if you do, please help me to find you. I want to know the truth, whatever it is. I want to give myself to the truth and live in truth. If you're the truth, I'm seeking you. You promised that all who seek you find you. So I claim that promise. Help me find you." And if you really mean that, I know he *will* help you find him.

Sal: That's fair enough. Like a scientific experiment, only my heart has to be in it. I'm putting myself in the test tube. Well, I *have* to know. I'll do it.

Chris: Congratulations, Sal. It's only a matter of time now.

Dialogue Nineteen

Concluding Dialogue

Sal: Good morning, Chris.

Chris: Good morning, Sal. Say, you look tired. Didn't you get much sleep last night?

Sal: You noticed, eh? Well, as a matter of fact, I didn't.

Chris: A party?

Sal: No. You'll never guess. I was up *thinking* half the night.

Chris: You're right. I never would have guessed *that*. What were you thinking about?

Sal: I was trying to be as honest with myself as I could be, and I discovered something about myself that I never knew before.

Chris: Good for you. What?

Sal: I asked myself what my real motives were for not believing in God, and in Christ, and in his Church.

Chris: That's a deep and honest question. What answer did you get?

Sal: It's kind of embarrassing. You know, I always thought I rebelled against believing because I was a freethinking kind of person, and I always thought faith was a blind leap in the dark, or just accepting whatever you're told without thinking for yourself—taking the lazy way out. I never wanted to believe for *that* reason. I had to decide for myself.

Chris: I know. I always admired you for that.

Sal: Well, you answered most of my questions about Christianity in the conversations we've been having, and I realized last night that I had no more good reasons for not believing.

Chris: So do you believe now?

Sal: I don't know. That's the embarrassing thing: I know now that I have no excuse left for not believing, and yet I still don't believe. So I asked myself why. I tried to be completely honest with myself. That's not easy, you know.

Chris: I know. Did you think it *was* easy?

Sal: I guess I used to think so. But I was wrong about that. It's hard. Very hard.

Chris: But it's also very, very precious. And it's worth the effort, because you'll find the truth if only you look long and hard and honestly.

Sal: How can you be so sure of that?

Chris: Jesus said so. Remember? "Seek and you shall find . . . everyone who seeks, finds."

Sal: Seek *what*? Find *what*? People seek plenty of things without finding them.

Chris: Yes, but he was talking about God. All who honestly seek the truth about God will find it—that's what he means.

Sal: I wish I could believe that as strongly as you do. But I see a lot of people who are seeking and not finding. In fact, I'm one of them!

Chris: I know. It takes time. But can we go back to last night? Can you tell me what happened when you asked yourself why you didn't believe? What answer did you find?

Sal: That's the embarrassing part. I don't think I *would* tell you if I didn't know you really care, and you understand me. I know you won't preach at me or put me down. Thanks for that.

Chris: Thanks for your thanks. But what's the embarrassing answer? Why won't you believe?

Sal: Because I'm afraid.

Chris: Of what? That it might not be true?

Sal: That's even more embarrassing: I'm afraid it might *be* true.

Chris: And why does that make you afraid?

Sal: Well, I think I want to control my life, and if I believe in God, that means letting God control my life. I don't want to boss anybody else around, but I want to be my own boss. I don't want God telling me what to do. Do you think I'm a terrible person because I feel that way?

Chris: No, Sal; I think you're a very honest person for admitting that to me, and, even more important, for admitting it to yourself.

Sal: Don't you believe your God hates me for running away from him?

Chris: Certainly not. He loves you no matter what. He's like the father of the Prodigal Son in the parable (Luke 15:11–32).

Sal: That's what makes it so hard. It feels like running away from home when your parents love you.

Chris: So you feel guilty about it?

Sal: I guess so.

Chris: There's a simple solution to that: turn around. That's what Jesus means by "repent": turn around. Run back to God. He won't condemn you, just as the father of the Prodigal Son didn't condemn him. We're all sinners, Sal, but some of us are sorry and saved sinners.

Sal: How do you handle the guilt if you've got all that sin?

Chris: Jesus handled it. He died to pay the price for all our sins—for *my* sins and for yours. That's the good news, the Gospel.

Sal: But you still have to try to keep the commandments.

Chris: Yes, but it's out of love, and that makes it a lot easier.

Sal: But you still sin.

Chris: Yes.

Sal: And you try not to.

Chris: Yes.

Sal: So you fail. You don't do what you try to do.

Chris: Right.

Sal: Well, I hate failure. I don't want to feel like a failure.

Chris: And therefore you won't try?

Sal: Right. If I don't try, I can't feel like I've failed.

Chris: Oh, Sal, you know you can't live that way. If you never try anything because you're afraid to fail, you'll hardly ever try anything at all in life.

Sal: It's not like that, Chris. I'm no coward. I'll try new things, and hard things too. I tried skiing last month for the first time, and I nearly broke my leg, but I'll try it again.

Chris: Then why not try faith in God?

Sal: I don't know.

Chris: Do you *want* to?

Sal: I don't know.

Chris: Suppose God appeared to you right now and made this deal with you: suppose he said, "Sal, I'll give you the gift of obeying my law. Will you take this gift?" What would you say?

Sal: I don't know. I don't think I would.

Chris: Good for you for being honest, at least. But *why* wouldn't you take God's deal?

Sal: I guess I just want to have the fun of sin without the guilt.

Chris: I think you already feel the guilt, deep down. And as far as giving up the fun is concerned, haven't you ever noticed how happy believers are?

Sal: You're happier than I am, anyway; I have to admit that. But we're just two people. That doesn't prove anything.

Chris: Facts are the best proof, right?

Sal: Right.

Chris: Then look at the facts. Here are your friends, who don't care about God. Their idea of fun is to get drunk or stoned, or to have sex outside of marriage. How happy are they, really, deep down? Can they bear to be alone with themselves? Don't they have to run away from themselves and keep themselves busy all the time with this frantic "fun" because they're really empty and unhappy inside? Come on, you know deep down that's so.

Sal: Maybe so, but some of your believing friends seem pretty dull and goody-goody. I can't be like that, and I don't want to.

Chris: Not all believers are like that. Many of us get a terrific thrill out of knowing God loves us and out of loving God and loving other people—loving their souls, not just their bodies.

Sal: It's all so mixed up . . .

Chris: No, it isn't! Be honest, Sal, just as you usually are. You know, deep down, that it's very, very simple, don't you? There's only one God, and he's got to be the only source of all happiness and all goodness. There's got to be much more happiness in God than in anything else, and the closer you get to him the happier you get. I think you know that.

Sal: Prove it to me.

Chris: No. You can't base your life on a proof. You have to base your life on a reality. On God.

Sal: But how can I know God for sure? I have to have facts. How can I know the facts about God?

Chris: Jesus Christ.

Sal: And how do I know Jesus? Show me Jesus.

Chris: I try to do that all the time. I wish I did it better.

Sal: You know, Chris, you do a pretty good job. Your arguments were all good, but the one that I can't escape is yourself. I know you really love me and care about me. That's Jesus in you, isn't it?

Chris: Of course it is. I'm just an ordinary kind of person, like an ordinary window. But the sun can shine through an ordinary window.

Sal: The Son of God, you mean?

Chris: Yes, the Son of God. Do you want his light in you, Sal?

Sal: I do. I do.

Chris: Then don't just tell me. Tell him.

Sal: I will.

Chris: *Now.* Don't put it off. It's too precious. It's the most important thing you'll ever do in your whole life. Don't let anything come between you and God, not even time. Don't put it off until another time.

Sal: You're right. Thanks for staying with me and saying those hard words to me. I needed them. All right, I guess the next step is between me and God. After I get that straightened out, can we talk some more?

Chris: As much as you like.

Recommended Reading

Best overall introduction to Christianity: C. S. Lewis, *Mere Christianity*

1. On reasons to believe:
   C. S. Lewis, "Man or Rabbit?" in *God in the Dock*

2. On faith and reason:
   Richard Purtill, *Thinking about Religion*, chap. 1
   Saint Thomas Aquinas, *Summa contra Gentiles*, I, 1–9

3. On arguments for the existence of God:
   Purtill, *Thinking about Religion*, chaps. 3 and 4
   Saint Thomas Aquinas, *Summa Theologica* vol. I, Q. 2, art. 3, "Whether God Exists?"

4. On science and religion:
   C. S. Lewis, "Religion and Science" in *God in the Dock*

5. On the problem of evil:
   C. S. Lewis, *The Great Divorce*
   C. S. Lewis, *The Problem of Pain*
   Purtill, *Thinking about Religion*, chap. 2
   Robert Farrar Capon, *The Third Peacock*
   Peter Kreeft, *Making Sense Out of Suffering*

6. On the identity of Jesus:
   Peter Kreeft, *Between Heaven and Hell*
   Peter Kreeft, *Socrates Meets Jesus*

7. On Jesus' Resurrection:
   Frank Morrison, *Who Moved the Stone?*
   William Craig, *The Son Rises*

8. On miracles:
   C. S. Lewis, *Miracles*
   Purtill, *Thinking about Religion*, chap. 5

9. On the Bible:
   George Martin, *Reading Scripture As the Word of God*
   C. S. Lewis, "Modern Theology and Biblical Criticism"
   in *Christian Reflections*
   Purtill, *Thinking about Religion*, chap. 6

10. On the meaning of death:
    Peter Kreeft, *Love Is Stronger Than Death*
    Sheldon Vanauken, *A Severe Mercy*
    C. S. Lewis, *A Grief Observed*

11. Life after death:
    Purtill, *Thinking about Religion*, chap. 9
    Plato, *Phaedo*

12. On the longing for Heaven:
    Peter Kreeft, *Heaven, The Heart's Deepest Longing*
    C. S. Lewis, *Surprised by Joy*
    C. S. Lewis, "The Weight of Glory"

13. On the nature of Heaven:
    Peter Kreeft, *Everything You Ever Wanted to Know
    about Heaven but Never Dreamed of Asking*
    Purtill, *Thinking about Religion*, chap. 10
    C. S. Lewis, *The Problem of Pain*, chap. 10

14. On Hell:
    C. S. Lewis, *The Great Divorce*
    C. S. Lewis, *The Problem of Pain*, chap. 8
    Charles Williams, *Descent into Hell*

15. On roads to Heaven and Hell:
    C. S. Lewis, *The Last Battle*
    John's Gospel
    Peter Kreeft, *Between Heaven and Hell*

16. On other religions:
    Purtill, *Thinking about Religion*, chap. 7
    Huston Smith, *The Religions of Man*

17. On relevance:
    C. S. Lewis, *Mere Christianity*
    C. S. Evans, *Existentialism*
    Thomas Howard, *Chance or the Dance?*
    Thomas Howard, *Dialogue with a Skeptic*
    Jean-Paul Sartre, *Existentialism and Human Emotions*
    Albert Camus, *The Stranger*

18. "Yes" or "no"?
    Pascal, *Pensées*

19. Conclusion:
    Saint Augustine, *Confessions*

Questions for Discussion

Dialogue One

1a. Do you agree that honesty is absolutely necessary?
 b. Why or why not?
 c. Imagine you were God; would you add anything to the answers you just gave?

2a. What do you think is the proper role of authority in our lives?
 b. What can it do?
 c. What can't it do?

3a. Do you fear questioning your faith?
 b. Why or why not?

Dialogue Two

1a. What do you think is the proper role of reason in relation to faith?
 b. What can it do?
 c. What can't it do?
 d. Why do you think someone else might give different answers to those questions?

2a. Do you believe there is objective truth?
 b. If so, do you think we can know any of it?
 c. If so, how?

3. How can Christianity claim to be objectively true (*does* it?) and yet not provable by the scientific method? (or *is* it?)

Dialogue Three

1. In your own words, what are Chris' five arguments for the existence of God?

2. If you accepted all five of these arguments, how much about God do they prove? What more does Christianity add about God?

3. Which argument do you think is the best one? Why?

4. Can you think of any other argument for the existence of God?

Dialogue Four

1. "The worst moment in the life of an atheist is the feeling of gratitude for life." What do you think this means?

2a. Give two or three examples of questions religion can answer and science can't.

 b. Give two or three examples of questions science can answer and religion can't.

3. Why does Chris think science needs religion to explain why science works at all?

4a. Do you think science can prove there is a God? Why or why not?

 b. Do you think science can prove there isn't a God? Why or why not?

5a. Do you think there could ever be a contradiction between science and Christianity?

 b. Why or why not?

Dialogue Five

1. Put in your own words the "problem of evil" and how it seems to prove the Christian God does not exist.

2. Put in your own words Chris' answer to this problem
    a. in terms of the *origin* of evil,
    b. in terms of the *purpose* in God allowing evil.

3. What does Jesus have to do with this last answer (2b)? What difference does Jesus make?

Dialogue Six

1. Why couldn't Jesus be a good man and not God?

2. Why couldn't Jesus be a bad man: a lunatic?

3. Why couldn't Jesus be a bad man: a liar?

4. What else could Jesus possibly be?

5. What difference does it make who Jesus is?

Dialogue Seven

1. What difference does it make whether Jesus really rose from the dead or not?

2. Why couldn't the story of Jesus' Resurrection be a myth or fairy tale that his disciples made up?

3. Why couldn't Jesus' disciples be mistaken about Jesus' Resurrection? Why couldn't it have been a hallucination?

Dialogue Eight

1a. If you subtract all the miraculous elements from Christianity, how much is left?
 b. What difference does the miraculous element make?

2a. What do you think is the strongest argument for *not* believing in miracles?

b. Do you think this argument can be answered? If so, how?

3a. Do you think most people decide whether or not to believe in miracles because they have or haven't seen any, or for some other reason?
 b. *What* other reason?
 c. Why do Christians believe in miracles?

4a. Can a scientist believe in miracles and still be a good scientist?
 b. Why or why not?

Dialogue Nine

1a. Do you think the miracle stories in the Bible really happened?
 b. Why or why not?

2a. Do you think the Bible is God's Word to us or our words about God?
 b. Why?

3a. How do you tell whether to interpret a passage in the Bible literally or symbolically? Give examples.
 b. Would you give a different answer for other books?

4. Put in your own words Chris' point about not confusing the question of *interpretation* with the question of *belief.*

Dialogue Ten

1a. Why does God let us die, according to Chris?
 b. Do you think this is a good answer or not?
 c. Why?

2a. If someone gave you a pill to make you immortal, would you take it or not?
 b. Why?

c. Why would Chris say eternal life in Heaven is good for us but not eternal life on earth?

3. What difference does Jesus make to the meaning of death?

Dialogue Eleven

1a. Is the question whether there is life after death or not important to you?
 b. Why or why not?
 c. What difference does it make to your life right now?

2. Put in your own words Chris' six arguments for life after death.

3a. Which of these six arguments seems strongest to you?
 b. Why?

4. Which of the following ideas would you agree with and why?
 a. You can prove there's no life after death.
 b. You can't prove or disprove life after death.
 c. You can prove that it's probable, or likely.
 d. You can prove that it's certain.
 e. You can be certain of it but not by logical proofs. (How?)

Dialogue Twelve

1a. Do you understand the feeling ("longing") Chris talks about?
 b. Do you think everyone can feel it?
 c. If so, why do you think we almost never talk about it?

2. Try to answer the question Chris asks at the very beginning: imagine you are God designing a Heaven of perfect happiness for yourself. Make two lists: What would be in your Heaven and what would not?

3a. How does the longing Chris talks about seem to prove the existence of Heaven? Put Chris' argument in your own words.

b. Evaluate this argument: compare it with Chris' six other arguments in Dialogue Eleven.

Dialogue Thirteen

1a. Do you think a strong faith in Heaven, hope for Heaven, and love of Heaven makes you stronger or weaker in your life on earth?

b. Why?

2a. What does Chris think we'll *do* in Heaven?

b. What do you think? What details would you add to Chris' answer?

3. Tell whether you think each of the following will be in Heaven or not and why: animals, plants, clocks, clothes, music, baseball, soldiers, law courts, broken legs, babies who died before birth, severely retarded people, angels, human emotions, sorrow, church buildings, sex, marriage, childbirth, food, cars, memory of earth, prayer.

Dialogue Fourteen

1a. What do you think is the strongest argument for not believing there is a Hell?

b. Do you think this argument can be answered?

c. If so, how?

2a. What do you think is the strongest argument for believing there is a Hell?

b. Do you think this argument can be answered?

c. If so, how?

3. Which of the items in question 3 in Dialogue 13 do you think will be in Hell?

Dialogue Fifteen

1a. Why do Christians believe the road to Heaven must be Jesus?
 b. Why do others believe the road to Heaven is just being good?
 c. How do you think you should decide which is right?

2. How could a Christian believe *both* that Jesus is the only way to Heaven *and* that some atheists, pagans, Hindus, Jews, or others could go to Heaven?

3. Imagine you were God. Try to arrange each of the following better than they are now:
 a. creating the world (could you design a better one?)
 b. leaving men and women free to choose good or evil (was that a mistake?)
 c. dealing with sin and evil after they sinned (how *did* God deal with sin according to the Bible?)
 d. the last judgment at the end of the world (could you get everyone to Heaven?)

4. Now think through the consequences of your choices in question 3. What would each of your arrangements lead to? (Take plenty of time to think about this. Discuss it with someone else.)

Dialogue Sixteen

1a. Why does Christianity's claim to be the one completely true religion seem unbelievable? (Sal's objection)
 b. Why do Christians believe this, then? (Chris' answer)

2. Imagine there are intelligent beings of different kinds on other planets. What do you think is Christ's relation to them, or their relation to Christ?

3. What does Christianity have that no other religion has?

4. What are some reasons for preferring theism to
   a. atheism,
   b. polytheism,
   c. pantheism?

Dialogue Seventeen

1. What "relevant" difference does Christ make to you and your life?

2. Why do you think other people often give different answers to that question?

3. What are Chris' answers to that question?

Dialogue Eighteen

1a. What, exactly, is the either/or, yes-or-no, "black-and-white" question?
 b. Why can't it be grey instead of "black or white"?

2a. Do you think Pascal's "wager" works as an argument to decide whether or not to believe?
 b. For whom would this argument work? For whom would it not work?

3a. What was Jesus talking about when he said "All who seek, find"?
 b. Do you believe this is true?
 c. Why or why not?
 d. What are the consequences of believing it?
 e. What are the consequences of not believing it?

Dialogue Nineteen

1. Do you think the reasons why most people choose not to be Christians are personal reasons like Sal's rather

than logical reasons? Do you think the decision to believe or not to believe is primarily a decision of the intellect or of the will?

2. What other reasons for hesitating do you think people have?

3. How convincing do you think Chris' reply to Sal is?

4a. What would you say to Sal if you were Chris?
  b. What would you say to Chris if you were Sal?

5. What do you think Sal will do now?